Baseball's Great Dynasties

THE

GIANTS

Baseball's
Great Dynasties
THE
GIANTS

Jim Kaplan

GALLERY BOOKS
An imprint of W.H. Smith Publishers Inc.
112 Madison Avenue
New York, New York 10016

Published by Gallery Books
A Division of W.H. Smith Publishers Inc.
112 Madison Avenue
New York, New York 10016

Produced by
Brompton Books Corp.
15 Sherwood Place
Greenwich, CT 06830

ISBN 0-8317-0627-9

Printed in Hong Kong

10 9 8 7 6 5 4 3 2 1

PICTURE CREDITS

All photos courtesy of UPI/Bettmann Newsphotos ex-
    cept the following:
Dwayne La Bakas: 54(both), 55(bottom left, bottom
    right), 56, 58(both), 63(all four), 64(both), 65(both),
    66.
National Baseball Library, Cooperstown, NY:
    12(top), 13, 14, 15, 16(left), 17(both), 18(both),
    20(top, bottom right), 21(both), 27(top left, top
    right), 32, 33(bottom), 34(top left, bottom), 45(top),
    51(top), 67(left).
    Ponzini Photography: 2, 68(both), 69, 70(left),
    73(top), 74(top), 77(right), endsheets.
Bruce Schwartzman: 3, 6, 7, 67(right), 70(right), 71,
    72(both), 74(bottom), 75(both).

ACKNOWLEDGMENTS

The author and publisher would like to thank the following people who helped in the preparation of this
book: Don Longabucco, the designer; Susan Bern-
stein, the editor; Rita Longabucco, the picture editor;
and Elizabeth McCarthy, the indexer.

Page 1: *Manager Leo Durocher with Whitey Lockman and Willie Mays during the 1954 championship season. Mays led the league in batting .345.*

Page 2: *A time-honored tradition – fans asking for autographs. Here, utility man Greg Litton obliges his admirers.*

Page 3: *Will Clark with his 23 homers and 111 RBIs helped the Giants reach the 1989 World Series.*

This page: *Shortstop Alvin Dark and second baseman Eddie Stanky, the Giants double play combination. Dark recorded the most double plays for a shortstop with 114 in 1951.*

Contents

Preface

There has never been a sports team more appropriately named than the Giants. To scrutinize their history is to believe in their moniker. Truly giants of baseball, they have spanned the game and, quite literally, spanned the continent – from New York to San Francisco. They've boasted the greatest manager of all time (John McGraw), the best all-around player (Willie Mays), and the most Hall of Famers (46). In Bobby Thomson, they've had perhaps the most spectacular one-game hero in baseball history.

The best World Series pitching performance? Simple: Christy Mathewson's three shutouts in 1905. What flair the Giants have played with: Mays and his basket catch, Carl Hubbell and his screwball, Mel Ott has his high-stepping swing. Some players have come straight out of the movies: Will "The Natural" Clark and Moonlight Graham from *Field of Dreams*. Others have performed like vaudeville veterans: poor Heinie Zimmerman chasing the Series-losing run across home plate, Terry Mulholland throwing his glove to first base, Casey Stengel wobbling around the bases to complete an inside-the-park home run with a loose shoe.

The Giants have had world-class talkers, too. Asked about the Dodgers, Bill Terry once said, "Are the Dodgers still in the league?" Nor should we overlook an unforgettable series of parks, ranging from

Below: *Brett Butler (2) stealing a base against the Mets. The fleet centerfielder led the league with 109 runs in 1988, his first year as a Giant.*

Opposite: *Sluggers Kevin Mitchell (l) and Will Clark, who are known as the "Pacific Sock Exchange."*

Right: *John McGraw, the Giants skipper from 1902 to 1932, hit .334 as a player. Considered baseball's best manager, he won 10 pennants and 3 world championships.*

Below: *The incomparable Willie Mays (24) batting in the 1951 World Series. Watching are Yankee catcher Yogi Berra and umpire Bill Summers.*

the historical (Polo Grounds) to the hysterical (Candlestick Park). A tragic as well as spectacular team, the Giants have won 17 pennants but only 5 World Series in the 20th century. Alas, some of the greatest goats in baseball history – Fred Snodgrass, Fred Merkle, Hank Gowdy – have worn Giant uniforms.

Indeed, the more we visit the Giants the more we come to equate them with the Red Sox. Like those baffling boys from Boston, the Giants dominated their circuit for roughly the first two decades of the modern era and have often fielded star-heavy lineups (the all-time Red Sox and Giant all-star teams, according to *The Baseball Research Journal*, are tops in their leagues). Both clubs have lost some especially heartbreaking Series – the Sox in 1946 and 1986, the Giants in 1912, 1924, and 1962. Neither team has won a world championship in ages

– the Giants since 1954, the Red Sox since 1918. Their styles have too often neglected speed and cunning and fallen prey to the sweet, siren call of the home run. Both teams have been victimized by arch rivals: the Red Sox by the damn Yankees, the Giants by the damn Dodgers.

Ah, but there's an important difference. A cloud of Calvinist gloom has settled over New England; some Red Sox fans seriously doubt their darlings will ever again capture the brass ring. Not so in California. After the Giants' Willie McCovey lined out to end the 1962 Series, a local radio station doctored the tape to end with the Giants winning. It sold well. Unlike the Back Bay booers, Giants fans are true believers with a sense of humor and a reservoir of hope.

All of which makes San Francisco a most satisfying club to watch – and a most pleasant one to chronicle.

Above: *Bobby Thomson is congratulated after hitting the "Shot Heard 'Round the World" to win the 1951 pennant. Huggers are Giant owner Horace Stoneham (l) and manager Leo Durocher (r).*

1. The New York Game

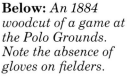

Below: *An 1884 woodcut of a game at the Polo Grounds. Note the absence of gloves on fielders.*

The Giants grew out of a New York baseball tradition second to none. That New York tradition is unparalleled in both myth and reality. For years people believed the sport was invented in 1839 by a West Point cadet named Abner Doubleday in Cooperstown, New York. Baseball actually evolved from several sources of English origin, ball games that include the informal game of rounders and that also led to the formal sport of cricket. Nonetheless, Cooperstown was selected as the site of the Hall of Fame when the Hall opened in 1939. According to a subsequent creation myth, New Yorker Alexander Cartwright unveiled modern baseball the day he umpired an 1846 game in Hoboken, New Jersey. According to the authoritative *Diamonds in the Rough*, however, "there is no evi-dence that he umpired this game" and modern rules had been in effect at least eight months at the time.

One tradition that remains undisputed is that Cartwright's Knickerbocker team did originate the modern rules, and Cartwright himself spread the game across the continent and ultimately to Hawaii; it's not for nothing that he's known as the "father of modern baseball." Another New Yorker, the British-born sportswriter Henry Chadwick, invented the box score. And 19th-century baseball fever ran highest in downstate New York, with games "on every available green plot within a 10-mile circuit of the city," according to one account.

Like rounders, baseball began as an eight-man game. In 1845 New York Knickerbocker D.L. Adams inserted him-

1

self as a short-outfielder, or "shortstop," and accounted for the one position change in baseball history. Eleven years later the Brooklyn Atlantics' Dickey Pearce became the first shortstop to study hitters and reposition himself around the infield; Pearce also invented the bunt. In the early 1860s Jim Creighton, a pitcher for the Brooklyn Excelsiors, was nearly unhittable.

During the Civil War the modern "New York game" eclipsed the "Massachusetts game," in which players ran around an irregular four-sided box and fielders threw the ball to hit baserunners and record outs. Because there were more soldiers from New York than Massachusetts in the Union Army, the New York version and its familiar trappings – including a diamond-shaped infield, foul lines, three strikes, and a tag or a throw to a base for an out – emerged from the struggle as our national pastime.

After America's first openly professional team, the Cincinnati Red Stockings, appeared in 1869, such colorfully named New York professional nines as the Bridegrooms and Superbas won championships. On June 14, 1870, another notable team, the Brooklyn Atlantics, beat the previously undefeated Red Stockings 8-7 in eleven innings; some baseball historians call that contest possibly the greatest game ever played. If the Atlantics weren't the best team of their time, they were certainly the best nicknamed. Among their numbers were Lip (The Iron Batter) Pike, a left-handed infielder and baseball's first Jewish player and manager; "Old Reliable" Joe Start, the first free-roaming first baseman; and John Chapman, an outfielder who made so many barehanded, over-the-shoulder catches that he was known as "Death to Flying Things." The same Chapman went on to manage the International League's Buffalo franchise, which in 1886-88 included second baseman Frank Grant, the best black player of the century.

But one team would eventually emerge as the class act, the pick of the crop, the giant among giants. The New York Giants were actually born upstate. When the Troy, New York, and Worcester, Massachusetts, clubs were expelled from the National Association after the 1882 season, the league looked toward major markets in New York and Philadelphia. A New York franchise – 18th in the National League – was awarded to manufacturer John B. Day when he purchased the Troy club. Day immediately divided his players between the two teams he now owned, the National League's Gothams and the American Association's Metropolitans. He situated both of their diamonds on a field just north of

Below: *In their first league game of the 1886 season, the Giants beat Boston in eleven innings.*

Top right: *These distinguished-looking gentlemen are New York Knickerbockers, the first team to play baseball under the modern rules. The man on the left in the top row is Alexander Cartwright, the "father of modern baseball." Cartwright headed to California for the gold rush, kept going, and spread the game as far as Hawaii.*

Bottom right: *The Polo Grounds in 1887.*

Central Park where *New York Herald* owner James Gordon Bennett played polo. That's why even the baseball field came to be known as the Polo Grounds.

At first the Metropolitans fared better than the Gothams, winning the American Association pennant in 1884 while their NL brethren finished fifth. The Metropolitans then lost to Providence three games to none in baseball's first championship series.

Since the NL club played in a more prestigious league and could charge higher ticket prices, Day decided to switch some of his major Mets to the Gothams for the 1885 season. Two of them were ace pitcher Tim Keefe and manager Jim Mutrie. The results were instantaneous. While the Metropolitans dropped to seventh, the Gothams (renamed "my giants" by Mutrie) had a .757 winning percentage – highest ever for a non-pennant-winner – and finished just two games behind Chicago in 1885. In 1888-89 the Giants captured pennants when Keefe and Mickey Welch won 116 games between them. Keefe won four more games as the Giants beat the American Association's St. Louis Browns, six games to four, in the 1888 championship.

Not even the burning-down of the original Polo Grounds in 1889 could keep the Giants from repeating as champions. They relocated temporarily to the St. George Cricket grounds on Staten Island and then to a second Polo Grounds at Coogan's Hollow. Today it's a housing project at Eighth Avenue between 155th and 157th Streets overlooking the Harlem River. A century ago the hollow was the last vestige of a farm the British crown granted one John Lion Gardiner in the 17th century. Harriett Gardiner Lynch, a great-granddaughter of the early Gardiners, inherited the farm and married the first Manhattan borough president, James J. Coogan. Hence, two names that would ring through Giant history: Coogan's Hollow and the outcropping of mica schist above it, Coogan's Bluff.

The 1889 Giants successfully defended their Series title, rebounding from a 3-1 deficit to beat the AA Brooklyn Bridegrooms six games to three. Ed "Cannonball" Crane won four times and first baseman Roger Connor drove in 12 runs.

Decimated by 13 defections to the rival Players League, the Giants finished sixth in 1890 while a Players League team played at an adjoining Coogan's Hollow location called Brotherhood Park. On May 12, a homer in the Polo Grounds landed in Brotherhood Park during a Players League game and fans in both places cheered the batter, Mike Tiernan. When the Players League folded at the end of the season, the Giants consolidated with the rival league's New York team and moved into their adjacent park at Coogan's Hollow and renamed it the Polo Grounds. In 1891 the Giants rose to third place. Unfortunately, Day couldn't afford to remain in the business and sold out in 1891 to financier Edward Talcott.

The club finished eighth in 1892 led by Pat Powers. Talcott quickly lured back former Giant John Montgomery Ward as

Above: *Manager Jim Mutrie (in civilian clothes) and the pennant-winning 1889 Giants. Originally called the Gothams, the team was renamed after Mutrie called them "my giants." In 1888–89 they were truly giants, winning two pennants when Tim Keefe (upper row, left) and Mickey Welch (lower row, second from right) combined for 116 wins.*

manager and they finished fifth in 1893, and second to Baltimore in 1894. That year pitchers Amos Rusie and Jouett Meekin tied for the league lead with 36 wins apiece. The National League was baseball's only major association at the time, but a kind of championship series was made possible when Pittsburgh sportsman William C. Temple offered a trophy for a series between the first- and second-place finishers. The Giants swept the Temple Cup series in four games, Meekin and Rusie winning two each and first baseman Jack Doyle batting .588. In a rare moment of Oriole pleasure – and a sneak preview of the Giants' future style – Oriole third baseman and later Giant manager John McGraw singled, reached second on a sacrifice, stole third, and scored on a single to deprive the Giants of a shutout.

Alas, that winter Talcott sold the club to Tammany Hall politician Andrew Freedman. An early day George Steinbrenner, Freedman abused player, opponent, fan, and official alike by running through 12 managers in eight years, barring critical journalists from the park, and fining Amos Rusie $200 after a 23-win season – angering him so much he sat out the next year. In a typical gesture, Freedman returned from a European vacation and blasted umpiring he hadn't seen. There was some justice: The Giants finished higher than seventh only once in his eight years of control.

In the middle of the 1902 season, while the National League was feuding with the upstart American League, the Giants got a break. John T. Brush, owner of the NL's Cincinnati Reds, bought the AL's Baltimore Orioles, released several prominent members to sign with the older league, sold the Reds and Orioles, and bought the Giants from the unpopular and increasingly harassed Freedman. Five former Orioles had joined the team, including some notable Hall of Famers. There was catcher Roger Bresnahan. There was pitcher Joe "Iron Man" McGinnity. And there was the pugnacious little manager named John Joseph McGraw.

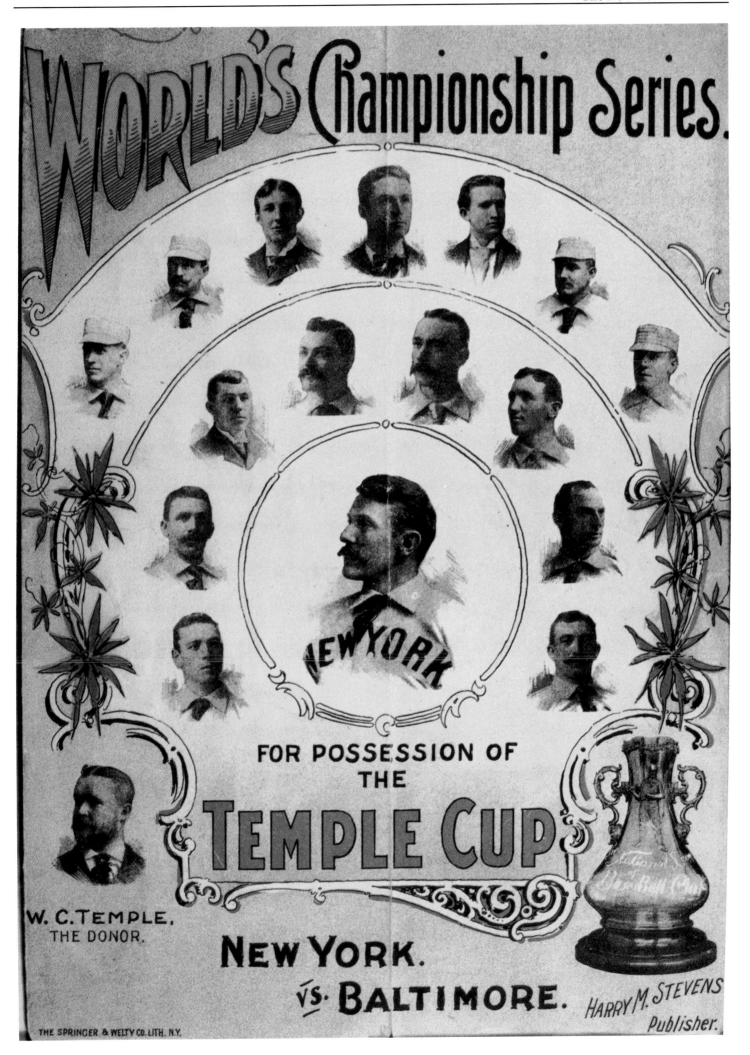

2. Welcome, Mr. McGraw

Below: *Roger Bresnahan, the first catcher to wear shinguards and a head protector.*

Below right: *Pitchers Joe "Iron Man" McGinnity (l) and Christy Mathewson flank manager John McGraw.*

A 5' 7" manager of the Giants? Why not? John McGraw had always played over his head. In 1891 a St. Louis Browns scout named Billy Gleason brought the 18-year-old, 155-pound third baseman to a tryout. "That little feller," snorted Chris Von der Ahe, the Brown's German-born owner, "take him over to the Fairgrounds track and make a hoss yockey out of him!" Instead Gleason took the little feller over to Baltimore, where he put in 10 crack seasons.

The 19th-century Orioles, a National League team in those days, and their resourceful manager Ned Hanlon would scratch and scheme and steal to win. A good example was the hit-and-run play, which McGraw and teammate Wee Willie Keeler were given credit for inventing. Perhaps they perfected it at one of Hanlon's 8 A.M. practices. Oh, that Oriole inventiveness! They'd build up the third-base foul line so that bunts stayed fair, and tilt the ground downhill from home to first base to give their speedy hitters a running start; hide balls in the long outfield grass to throw in when hits soared over their heads; flash mirrors at opposing pitchers and hitters; sprawl on the ground faking injuries on close pitches; bury cement in front of home plate and swing down on balls to hit high-bouncing "Baltimore chops." One of

McGraw's favorite tactics was to throw his hip at opponents as they rounded third. He sometimes grabbed their belts, a tactic that worked until Pete Browning unbuckled his belt and left it dangling in McGraw's hand as he sped home.

McGraw hit .300 or better 10 times, played on National League championship teams in 1894-96 and Temple Cup winners in 1896-97, and retired with a .334 average after a 16-year playing career. Yet he was to become even better known as a manager. McGraw took over the Orioles in 1899 and jumped with them to the fledgling American League in 1901. When AL president Ban Johnson sided with the umpires in their endless disputes with McGraw, he jumped back to the National and took over the Giants on July 19, 1902.

In 1903, his first full season, the Giants won 36 more games than they had the previous year and finished a strong second to Pittsburgh. Roger Bresnahan batted .350, while Iron Man McGinnity won a league-high 31 games, followed by teammate Christy Mathewson – whom McGraw had switched off part-time infield duty – with 30 wins. Still better things were to come.

In 1904 the Giants were fighting mad. McGraw made sure of that. In spring training a judge in Mobile, Alabama issued arrest warrants for the entire team after they beat a hometown umpire into uncon-

sciousness. The Giants left town just in time. Goaded by McGraw, who supervised their diet, hours, and off-field activities, they won a team-record 106 games and the pennant. McGinnity (35-8) led the league with a 1.61 earned run average and Mathewson (33-12) had an NL-high 212 strikeouts. That was satisfaction enough for McGraw. Still railing against Ban Johnson, he refused to play the World Series against the "bush" American League.

In 1905 McGraw relented. First, Mathewson led the Giants to another National League crown while leading the league with 31 wins, a 1.27 ERA, 206 strikeouts, and 8 shutouts. McGraw treated Mathewson's every start – and all the other Giant games, for that matter – like "Gunfight at O.K. Corral." "His very walk across the field in a hostile town was a challenge to the multitude," wrote Grantland Rice. Before a series on the road, McGraw would blast his upcoming opponents and wire ahead to police for extra protection. The newspapers would print the quotes and telegrams and whip the crowd into a frenzy.

The public had reacted furiously to the Giants' spurning a World Series in 1904. This time, with the Series declared a permanent institution, they played. McGraw dressed his team in black for the post-season showdown, and the AL champion Philadelphia Athletics were so intimidated they fell in five games.

But the star of the Series wasn't McGraw.

Above left: *Christy Mathewson. One of the greatest pitchers and best-loved sports figures of the 1900–15 period, he won 373 games and dazzled hitters with his "fadeaway" (screwball). "To me," said Matty's mentor and friend, John McGraw, "he was pretty much the perfect type of pitching machine. . . . There was never another pitcher like Mathewson." Nor another personality. Big Six starred in vaudeville, wrote inspirational books for boys and played checkers exhibitions blindfolded. Gassed in World War I, he developed tuberculosis and died during the 1925 World Series. In a rare tribute, players on both teams wore black armbands.*

Left: *A Giant at the beginning and end of his career (1892–1910), the 5'4½", 140-pound "Wee Willie" Keeler had 2,932 hits. "I hit 'em where they ain't," said Keeler, a contact hitter supreme. Wee Willie hit 'em well enough to run up a 44-game hitting streak while batting .424 in 1897.*

Above right: *The 1904 New York Giants, who set a club record with 106 wins and took the National League pennant. Unfortunately, manager McGraw (c) refused to play the "bush" American League in the World Series.*

Right: *Lefty Rube Marquard tied a major league record by winning 19 straight games in 1912 and would have been awarded a 20th under today's scoring rules. Purchased from Indianapolis in 1908 for a then-record $11,000, he was known as the "$11,000 lemon" when he turned in mediocre records his first 2 seasons. Marquard rebounded to become a 20-game winner in 1911–13 and no-hit the Dodgers on April 15, 1915. A flashy-dressing sophisticate, he married a Broadway actress and performed on stage himself.*

It was Mathewson, his polar opposite in size and temperament. At 6′ 1½″ and 195 pounds, Mathewson was called "Big Six." A gentlemanly, one-time Bucknell student, he had starred in three sports and been class president and a member of the glee club and two honor societies. He was also the kind of astute baseball man McGraw liked. Noticing that batters could "read" heavy-spinning curveballs, Matty developed a reverse-breaking "fadeaway," forerunner of the screwball. Now, in his fifth full season and first World Series at age 25, he would show just how perfect it had become.

Game one: Mathewson blanks the A's 3-0 on four hits while his teammates, playing McGrawesque baseball, steal four bases. Game two: Philadelphia rebounds to win by the same score. Game three: Pitching on two days' rest, Mathewson throws another four-hitter and wins 9-0; the winners steal five bases. Game four: McGinnity wins a 1-0 thriller, and the Giants take a 3-1 lead in games. Game five: Just two days after his previous start, Mathewson closes out the Series with a nifty 2-0 six-hitter.

Mathewson's sustained excellence – three complete-game shutouts in six days, 18 strikeouts, one walk, and no runs in 27 innings – may never be matched in the fall classic. Nor, in all likelihood, will the 1905 Series' mark of five shutouts in five games.

The Giants were suddenly kings of Broadway, McGraw the buddy of actors and fighters. The team was also due for a let-down, and it came all too quickly. Though they won 96 games in 1906, they finished a distant second to the Chicago Cubs and their major league record of 116 victories. The Giants slipped to fourth, at 82-71, in 1907. Then followed the unkindest cut of all.

In 1908 the Giants were locked in a tight race with the Cubs. In a critical game, on September 23, the Giants appeared to win when Al Bridwell singled with runners on first and third to break a 1-1 tie in the last of the ninth. However, Cub second baseman Johnny Evers noticed that Fred Merkle, the Giant on first, hadn't bothered to touch second. Evers procured a ball – historians dispute whether it was the ball Bridwell hit – touched second, and appealed the hit. At 10 P.M. home plate umpire Hank O'Day ruled Merkle out and the game a tie. When Chicago and New York finished in a dead heat for the pennant, the tied game was re-scheduled for October 8. The Cubs won 4-2 to take the pennant and went on to beat the Tigers in the World Series.

The famous Merkle blunder was a double blow for Mathewson. First, Merkle cost Big Six a win in the September 23 game; in the tie-breaking game, a Giant outfielder's re-fusal to follow Matty's instructions and play deep resulted in Joe Tinker's critical triple. But Merkle paid even more dearly. Normally a heads-up player, he was now nicknamed Bonehead Merkle; in fact, the use of "boner" to mean foolish mistake was popularized in his honor.

There followed distant third- and second-place finishes in 1909 and 1910. Typically, McGraw's Giants rebounded dramatically. Early in 1911 a fire destroyed the Polo Grounds' wooden leftfield pavilion. Owner John T. Brush, a dynamic man despite rheumatism and a disease called locomotor ataxi that kept him confined to a wheel-chair, decided to rebuild the entire park in concrete and steel. The result: Polo Grounds IV, an impressive, massive oval. Only 256 feet down the rightfield line and 277 in left – overhanging decks built a decade later actually reduced the distance on high flies – the dimensions invited dra-matic home runs. A full 433 feet to center – the distance would increase to 483 in later years – the spacious outfield beckoned for long-running catches. Young boys and old men sat outside the park on Coogan's Bluff, where they could see the centerfielder, left-fielder, second baseman, and scoreboard, and guess what was happening inside. Who knew what wonders awaited?

Like their home park, the 1911 Giants rose phoenix-like from the ashes. Getting 26 wins from Mathewson, 24 from Rube

Left: *A popular Giant second baseman in 1907–16 and 1918–20, "Laughing Larry" Doyle was a solid performer who led the league in doubles, triples, hits, and average, batted .290 and stole 298 bases. "It's great," he said, "to be young and a Giant."*

Marquard, and 13 homers and a league-leading 25 triples from second baseman Larry Doyle, the Giants pulled ahead of Chicago in early September en route to the first of three straight pennants. McGraw was as active and original as ever, calling pitches from the bench and using relievers before these practices became common-place. He even outfitted a mentally unba-lanced man from Kansas, Charles Faust, as a good-luck mascot. McGraw was now known as "Little Napoleon," and he played

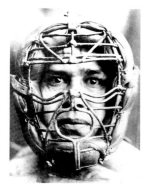

Top: *Manager John McGraw skippered the team to three consecutive pennants from 1911 to 1913.*

Above: *John "Chief" Meyers. A full-bloodied Indian, he caught for the 1909–15 Giants.*

Right: *Fred "Bonehead" Merkle.*

the part like a trouper. "The nickname is well founded," wrote Douglass Wallop, "in terms of both his autocratic methods and the impression he gave as he directed the team from the third base coach's box – a short, stumpy figure assuming an attitude that always seemed to be the same as the years passed, even when the pot-belly became more pronounced and the hair turned gray and then white, his face became grizzled and the small eyes seemed to grow even smaller as they became hemmed in with wrinkles."

But not even McGraw could control all events. In the 1911 Series, Frank Baker earned the nickname Home Run Baker when he hit two round-trippers, and the Athletics beat the Giants four games to two. They even bested Mathewson in two of his three starts.

The Giants were back in 1912, led again by Mathewson (23 wins) and Marquard (26 wins and a 19-game winning streak). Their Series opponents, the Boston Red Sox, boasted one of the greatest defensive outfields in history – rightfielder Harry Hooper, centerfielder Tris Speaker, and leftfielder Duffy Lewis. Smokey Joe Wood added one of the finest pitching years (34-5, 35 complete games, 10 shutouts, 1.91 ERA) ever.

If McGraw could manage, he could also over-manage. As his game one starter in New York he chose neither Mathewson nor Marquard, but rookie Jeff Tesreau. "McGraw had a hunch that Tesreau might surprise the Red Sox in the opener and then Mathewson would take over in Boston," Joseph Durso wrote in *Casey and Mr. McGraw*. "But his hunch wore thin . . . " Wood out-dueled Tesreau 4-3. Mathewson was indeed ready for game two, but the Giants committed five errors and were lucky to escape with a 6-6 tie in a game called because of darkness.

Rube Marquard beat Buck O'Brien 2-1 in the second completed game, but hardly anyone knew it at the time. The game ended in a thick mist, when Boston's Forest (Hick) Cady hit a line drive to rightcenter field with two men on base in the last of the ninth. Josh Devore made a running catch and didn't stop until he entered the Giants' dugout. Many of the Fenway Park faithful, however, thought the ball had whistled by him and two BoSox had come home for a 3-2 victory. After the game the umpires told the writers that Devore had caught the ball. Game to the Giants. Frustration for the Red Sox. Near riot in Kenmore Square. Wood and Hugh Bedient outpitched Tesreau and Mathewson 3-1 and 2-1 to give Boston a two-game lead. Marquard and Tesreau won 5-2 and 11-4 to even the Series

at 3-3. The stage was set for the deciding game in Boston. It proved to be one of the greatest in World Series history.

The Giants scored a run off Bedient in the third but were robbed of another in the sixth when Hooper dived into the temporary right-center bleachers to make a barehanded catch of a sure homer. In the seventh Boston manager – first baseman Jake Stahl reached on a Texas leaguer between three Giant fielders. After walking Heinie Wagner on four pitches, starter Mathewson then surrendered a double off the third-base bag to pinch hitter Olaf Henriksen, and the score was tied.

In the tenth inning Red Murray doubled, Fred Merkle singled him home, and the Giants had a 2-1 lead. Then came perhaps the most frustrating half-inning in their history. Pinch-hitting for reliever Wood, Clyde Engle led off the bottom of the tenth with a routine fly to center. The Giants' Fred Snodgrass camped under it, raised his glove, seemed to catch the ball – and dropped it, allowing Engle to reach second. Following the game on an electric scoreboard in a Los Angeles theater, Snodgrass's mother fainted and had to be carried out. His obituaries would mention the "$30,000 muff" (the difference between the winning and losing team shares). The obit writers never mentioned that Snodgrass subsequently made a spectacular catch of a Hooper driver. (Engle tagged up and went to third.) The nay-sayers further neglect to note that what happened next was more pivotal still. After Steve Yerkes walked, putting runners on first and third with one out, Mathewson induced Speaker to hit an easy foul fly down the first-base line. Accounts differ on what followed. According to some, Mathewson called off first baseman Merkle, who was closest to the ball, by shouting "Chief!" to catcher Chief Meyers. Others say either Speaker or the

Boston bench distracted Merkle. In either case, the snakebit Merkle froze and the ball dropped safely. Given new life, Speaker singled to tie the score and advanced to second on the throw home while Yerkes sped to third. The Giants had made one muff too many: After Duffy Lewis was intentionally passed to load the bases, Larry Gardner hit a long sacrifice fly to win the Series.

If the loss wasn't stunning enough to the Giants, owner John T. Brush died on a train to California during the off-season. Control of the team went to Brush's widow and daughters, with a son-in-law named Harry Hempstead installed as president. Control of the business end went to club secretary John B. Foster. The result was a front-office feud until McGraw gained control a few years later.

In 1913 the Giants were back for a third

Top: *The Giants pose at the Polo Grounds during the 1912 World Series.*

Above: *Game one starters Joe Wood (left) and Jeff Tesreau. McGraw gambled by starting Tesreau over better-known pitchers, and Boston's Wood beat him.*

Above:
Philadelphia's Frank "Home Run" Baker is out at third in the 1913 Series opener. Baker wasn't out often: He batted .450 and drove in a Series-high 7 runs while the Athletics beat the Giants in five games. A nasty nemesis, he had homered twice against New York in the 1911 Series to earn his nickname.

straight Series. It was also their third against the Athletics and the last time McGraw would face Philadelphia manager Connie Mack. Before the Series a fortune teller sat in the A's dugout and told Mack, "All signs are favorable."

They should have been. Though New York rounded up the usual suspects – Mathewson (25-11), Marquard (23-10), and Doyle (73 RBIs) – they also had a suspect lineup because Snodgrass and Merkle ended the season with leg injuries. McGraw inserted utility man Tillie Shafer for Snodgrass and hid Merkle in the number eight batting position. Alas, Home Run Baker hit a two-run tater and the A's won the opener, 6-4. Things only got worse when Baker piled up seven RBIs and Wally Schang six, and Chief Bender beat the Giants twice in a five-game Series. In the fourth game McGraw's first-base coach and old pal, Wilbert Robinson, sent a runner to second only to see him thrown out. Robinson said McGraw had ordered the steal, McGraw denied that and fired Robinson to end a 20-year friendship. Robinson later became manager of the Dodgers, and the teams fought as bitterly as their skippers.

If McGraw felt fit to be tied, he was probably fit to be whipped in 1914, when the Miracle Braves passed the Giants on September 8, won 34 of their last 44 to take the pennant, then whipped the Athletics four straight in the Series. And 1915 was even worse: The Giants slipped to dead last, while Mathewson went 8-14 in his final full season as a Giant and Marquard was traded to the Dodgers.

But McGraw was nothing if not resourceful. His greatest gift may have been evaluating talent – discovering rookies others had overlooked or digging veterans off the scrap heap for one last hurrah. The Giants rose to fourth in 1916. By 1917 only three regulars remained from the 1915 club, yet New York finished first by 10 games! Who *were* these guys? Well, there were a couple of scratch .300 hitters, centerfielder Benny Kauff (who in 1915 had been the "Ty Cobb of the Federal League") and leftfielder George Burns. There were league assist leaders Artie Fletcher at short and Heinie Zimmerman at third. Zimmerman led the league with 102 RBIs, and Dave Robertson had an unmatched 12 homers. Ferdie Schupp was 21-7 in his best season. And Slim Sallee, late of the Cardinals, went 18-7, with a league-leading 4 saves. In short McGraw had molded another champion.

In the 1917 Series against the White Sox, however, Little Napoleon again left himself open for second-guessing. He chose Sallee over Schupp in the opener, and Chicago's Eddie Cicotte outdueled him 2-1. In the second game Schupp was knocked out in the second inning, and the White Sox coasted to a 7-2 victory. Rube Benton and Schupp shut out Chicago over the next two games, but McGraw stayed with Sallee too long in the fifth game. Before reliever Pol Perritt could put out the fire in the eighth, the White Sox scored three times to break up a 5-5 deadlock and win 8-5. In the finale the Giants did far more damage than their manager. With no score in the fourth, the Giants made two errors to put White Sox on first and third. Then Happy Felsch hit back to the mound, and Eddie Collins was trapped off third. In the ensuing rundown, though, Zimmerman chased Collins across the plate. The frustrated third sacker had no choice: There was no one covering home but umpire Bill Klem. Chicago scored 3 runs in the inning and won 4-2.

As McGraw left the field Chicago manager Pants Rowland tried to console him. "Mr. McGraw," he said, "I'm sorry you had to be the one to lose." McGraw looked up quickly and snapped, "Get away from me, you damned busher."

But don't get the wrong impression. The Giants may have won only one of five Series and suffered some real heartbreaks at this point in their history, but they were still kings of New York, led by the king of managers. Surely more championships lay ahead. Larry Doyle, a Cub in 1917, must have been glad to return to New York the following season. "It's great," Doyle once said, "to be young and a Giant."

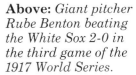

Above: *Giant pitcher Rube Benton beating the White Sox 2-0 in the third game of the 1917 World Series.*

Left: *Chicago's Joe Jackson scoring in the second game.*

Overleaf: *Eddie Collins of the White Sox is tagged out in the fourth game. In the finale, however, he scored the go-ahead run when he was chased across an unguarded home plate by Giant third baseman Heinie Zimmerman.*

3. The Battle of Broadway

The times, they were a-changing. Because so many major league players had been drafted to serve in World War I and baseball had been classified non-essential, the 1918 season was concluded by Labor Day. As the Giants began a streak of three consecutive second-place finishes, the Brush estate sold the team to a broker named Horace A. Stoneham, who was little-known in baseball circles but proclaimed himself "a Giant man all my life and an admirer of Mr. McGraw." In yet another change, the Polo Grounds opened its gates to Sunday baseball in 1919.

But the biggest threat to the status quo were the American League's upstart New York Yankees. In 1921, with the Yankees and Giants sharing the Polo Grounds while the Yankees built their own pleasure palace across the Harlem River, both teams won pennants – the Yankees' first, the Giants' seventh. The Yankees' Babe Ruth had his best all-around season, hitting .378 and leading the AL with 59 homers, 171 RBIs, 144 walks, 177 runs, an .846 slugging percentage, and a .512 on-base percentage. As for the Giants, dynasty-builder McGraw acquired Casey Stengel, Emil "Irish" Meusel, and Johnny Rawlings from the Phillies, switched Frisch from second to

third, and put Rawlings at second. Seven regulars hit over .300 topped by Frisch's .341, and first baseman George "Highpockets" Kelly's 23 homers led the league. McGraw had still other worthies, like shortstop Dave Bancroft, who fielded up a storm and hit for the cycle one game, as well as a pitching staff led by Art Nehf (20-10).

McGraw's managing had never seemed surer. Seven and a half games behind Pittsburgh on August 24, the Giants won the first of a five-game series with the leaders when McGraw ordered Kelly to swing at a 3-0 pitch with the bases loaded. He responded by homering off Babe Adams. "Kelly couldn't hit Adams's curveball if he stood at the plate all day," McGraw explained to a dumbstruck future manager, Casey Stengel. "But on this one pitch Adams has to come in with his fastball. And since it would be the only fastball Kelly would get all day, I let him hit it." When Kelly congratulated McGraw after the game, he replied. "If my brains hold out, we might even win this pennant." They did, and the Giants did. New York won the rest of that Pirate series and swept inexorably toward first.

But there was no question which Polo Grounds club led in attention. It was Ruth whose home run bat ushered in the lively ball era and proved to be precisely the tonic baseball needed in the wake of the Black Sox scandal. Ruth and the Yankees out-

drew the Giants, outwon them (98-94), and generally outraged them. So on to the 1921 World Series – alias, the Battle of Broadway.

The Series – baseball's last using a best-of-nine games format, first between two teams from the same city, and first in a single stadium – started fast but not well for the landlords. In only 98 minutes Yankee submariner Carl Mays five-hit the Giants 3-0 while Mike McNally stole McGraw's style by stealing home. Waite Hoyt allowed only two hits and the Yankees won again by the same score. By the middle of the third inning of the third game, the Giants were down two games and four runs and hadn't scored at all. But they rallied for four runs in their half of the third and won going away 13-5, with 20 hits off 4 Yankee pitchers. Ruth got his first of 15 Series homers in game four, but the Giants won, 4-2.

The Yankees and Hoyt won game five 3-1, and Ruth made the biggest news. First, the big guy beat out a bunt to start a two-run fourth. Then he developed an abscess on his left elbow and was disabled except for one pinch-hitting appearance for the rest of the Series. The Ruth-less Yankees bowed out 8-5, 2-1, and 1-0.

McGraw had never been happier. "I signaled every pitch to Ruth," he said. "We

Left: *Frankie Frisch, the second baseman on pennant-winning Giant teams of 1921–24. Claiming he "never hit a home run when a single would win the game," the switch-hitting "Fordham Flash" had a league-leading 223 hits in 1923.*

Above left: *A Giant outfielder in 1921–23, Casey Stengel learned from the master, McGraw, and later became a record-setting manager with the Yankees.*

Above right: *Dave "Beauty" Bancroft, star Giant shortstop in 1920–23.*

pitched only nine curves and three fastballs to Ruth during the entire Series. All the rest were slowballs, and of the twelve of those, eleven set him on his ear." And the Series set McGraw to tinkering rather than resting: Two months later he strengthened the team by acquiring third baseman Heinie Groh from the Reds. Groh became a colorful and eccentric Giant.

The twenties were really roaring now, and the McGraw-Ruth rivalry would earn a place of honor beside bathtub gin, Jack Dempsey, Bobby Jones, Bill Tilden, and Charles Lindbergh. Would the Babe and the emerging power game overwhelm McGraw's pesky, punchy playing style? Or would Little Napoleon and his "little ball" – with its brazen steals, intricate signals, and sophisticated defenses (a precursor of "Billy Ball") – stay on top?

In 1922 the Yanks and Giants repeated as pennant winners, but Ruth limped to their second confrontation. Against the orders of baseball Commissioner Kenesaw Mountain Landis, Ruth and teammate Bob Meusel had joined a barnstorming tour after the 1921 Series. Their punishment: suspension until May 20, 1922. Ruth then suffered one of the worst slumps of his career, although a .315 average, 35 homers, and 96 RBIs would have sufficed for most players. Forecasting a one-sided Series, the Yankees won the AL by a single game, while the Giants, led by Frisch's .327 hit-

ting, 31 stolen bases, and endless hustle, won by seven.

Nonetheless, the Series set records for hype and sideshow. A skywriting plane passed overhead at the opener, trailing the message "Hello USA. Call Vanderbilt 7200." For the next five hours the number – for the switchboard at Vanderbilt Hotel – was the most called in America. The Series was on radio for the first time. And everyone from George M. Cohan to John J. Pershing came to watch.

When McGraw switched tactics and went for the big inning, the Giants scored all their runs in one inning three times and won four straight games. Frisch hit .471 and one of McGraw's reclamation projects, Jack Scott, threw a shutout. Ruth drove in all of one run, got all of two hits, and was humiliated by McGraw, off as well as on the field. Nicked by a pitch during game two, Ruth bumped third baseman Groh and traded insults with the Giants bench. After the game he and teammate Bob Meusel barreled into the Giant clubhouse. Just as a fight was about to begin, McGraw barged into the room and ordered the Ruth-Meusel tag team to "get out and stay out." They did. The only other news of note was the decision by umpires George Hildebrand and Bill Klem the previous day to call a 3-3 game on account of "darkness" at 4:40 P.M. Besieged by angry fans, Commissioner Landis – who hadn't made the call – ordered

Above right: *Casey Stengel slides home with the winning run – an inside-the-park homer – in game one of the 1923 Series. A pad in his shoe shifted as he rounded second, causing him to stumble all the way home.*

Right: *Game three starters Art Nehf (l) and Sam Jones. The Giants' Nehf bested Jones 1-0 on Stengel's second colorful homer (this time he thumbed his nose at the Yankees while rounding third).*

the proceeds of $120,000 turned over to charities and veteran groups.

There was even more hoopla – this time more deservedly so – when the New York teams met for a third consecutive curtain call in 1923. The Yankees were now ensconced in their Bronx palace, the magnificent Yankee Stadium. Getting a full season of play, Ruth shone (.393, 41 homers, 130 RBIs), and a new kid on the block, Lou Gehrig, batted a .423 in 13 late-season games. The Yankees asked permission to activate him for the Series – technically he had been brought up too late – and McGraw magisterially refused.

Over in Harlem, the Polo Grounds were increased to a 53,000-seat capacity and double-decked in right-center and left-center. McGraw, scratched and scrounged more than usual to win his 9th pennant in 21 years. When Bancroft came down with pneumonia, McGraw promoted Travis Jackson from Little Rock. With superior range, a strong arm, and a .291 bat, Jackson would play 15 seasons for the Giants and make the Hall of Fame. When the pitching staff faltered, McGraw bought Jack Bently (13-8) from Baltimore. "A collection of misfits," wrote the *New York Times*.

New Yorkers were divided on Series favorites. Fanny Brice picked the Yankees. Willie Hoppe chose the Giants. By now strong loyalties were being formed, based largely on class. They would change as the team's fortunes changed, but in the early 1920s the Giants represented the Establishment and the Yankees the Underdog. "It was easy to tell a Yankee fan from a Giant fan," said a man who grew up in New York at the time. "When I took the Ninth Avenue 'El,' the only public transportation stopping at both parks, the brokers in straw hats would get off at the Polo Grounds. You never saw people like that going to Yankee Stadium."

"Will McGraw stop the greatest hitter in baseball?" the *Times* pondered. "Will Ruth redeem his failure of 1922 and step forward as the outstanding star of the Yankees?" Ah, but a third figure made the marquee. With the opener tied 4-4 in the ninth, Giant veteran Casey Stengel lined a hit over the shortstop's head and kept running when the ball rolled to the deepest part of the stadium. As he rounded second, a pad in his shoe shifted, affecting his gait. Panting and gimping, the 33-year-old Stengel raced the ball for the plate. Casey won, sliding home with the game-winning inside-the-park-homer, then half-rising and waving his hand comically at the crowd. It was the eighth straight win over the Yankees in post-season competition.

The Yankees bolted upright in game two, winning 4-2 on Ruth's two homers. "The Ruth is mighty," wrote New York columnist Heywood Broun, "and shall prevail."

But in game three the Giants – well, Stengel, anyway – prevailed. Casey smote a Sam Jones pitch into the rightfield bleachers in the seventh and paused on his way around the bases to thumb his nose at the Yankee bench. It was the game's only run, and fun.

But one player a team does not make – unless maybe it's the Bambino. Ruth hit safely in all 6 games and finished with a .368 average and 3 homers, and the Yankees won the Series 4 games to 2. Poor John McGraw. "I just can't see that third [straight] World Series victory," he said prophetically. "It just don't seem to be my good fortune. I guess that's one ambition I'll never have fulfilled."

Below: *The crowd at the 1923 World Series.*

4. Is There Life After McGraw?

John McGraw would not even win one more world championship. Nor would he run the Giants as effectively any more. A new breed of ballplayer – one less receptive to Little Napoleon's dictatorial ways – had entered the Giant scene.

After the 1923 Series, McGraw traded shortstop Dave "Beauty" Bancroft and outfielders Casey Stengel and Bill Cunningham to the Boston Braves for pitcher Joe Oeschger and outfielder Billy Southworth. McGraw piously explained away the trade – which looked like a steal for Boston – by claiming that he wanted to help the Braves' ailing president, his old friend Christy Mathewson. Others felt McGraw was more interested in trading Stengel, who had upstaged him during the Series.

But McGraw wasn't willing to go down without a fight. After missing a spring training game because of illness, he was furious when he learned that the Giants had left the field in a tie game because the scorekeeper incorrectly hung a "9" instead of an "8" beside the opponents' column. Why was he so excited about a mere exhibition game? a reporter asked innocently enough. "What difference does it make?" McGraw roared rhetorically. "I don't care whether it was an exhibition game or a World Series! These people down here look up to the major league clubs. What do you think they are going to say when they read the papers tomorrow morning and see what a lot of incompetents I have travelling around with me?"

If McGraw inspired fear, he also inspired respect. The little genius had a cadre of loyalists scouting up prospects around the country, and in 1924 they paid off. Freddy

Right: *Pictured here are the Giants who were playing their fourth consecutive Series in 1924. Seated from left: Frankie Frisch, Hughie Jennings, Art Nehf. Standing from left: Pep Young, George "Highpockets" Kelly, Frank Snyder, Emil "Irish" Meusel, Rosy Bill Ryan.*

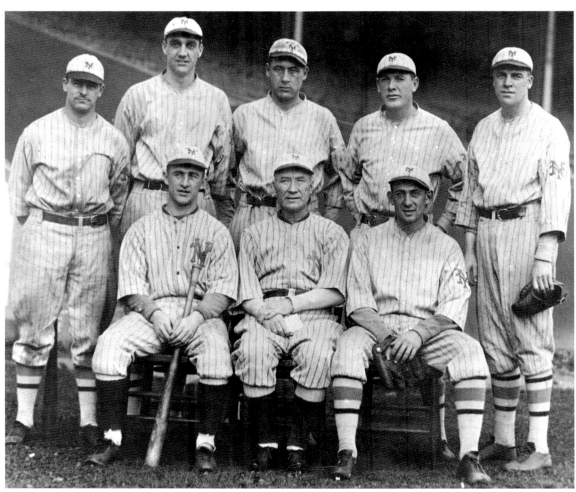

Lindstrom, an 18-year-old third baseman discovered at Chicago's Loyola Academy, made the club. So did another rookie and future Hall of Famer, first baseman Bill Terry. (McGraw had wisely insisted that Terry give up pitching in the minors.) Meanwhile, Highpockets Kelly led the league with 136 runs batted in and had 21 homers and 37 doubles, while Bentley (16-5) Virgil Barnes (16-10), Art Nehf (14-4), and Hugh McQuillan (14-8) anchored a deep pitching staff. Despite a grim season on the public relations front – outfielder Jimmy O'Connell and coach Cozy Dolan were expelled from baseball for attempting to bribe a Phillie player – the Giants won their tenth and last pennant under McGraw.

Alas, the 1924 Series may have been his greatest disappointment. In the seventh and deciding game the great man was embarrassed, outmanaged and certainly outlucked. With the Series tied at three games apiece, Bucky Harris, the Washington Senators' "boy" manager, maneuvered successfully to get Terry's .500-hitting bat out of the Giant lineup. Harris warmed up Curly Odgen, an undistinguished right-hander. Ogden faced two batters and was replaced by left-handed George Mogridge. When the left-handed-hitting Terry came to bat, would McGraw replace him with a right-hander? Not the first time up. Not the second time either. But the third time, with the Senators leading 1-0 in the sixth, McGraw pinch hit Irish Meusel for the hit he hoped would even the score. Having set the trap, Harris sent in right-handed Firpo Marberry. Meusel did drive in a run with a sacrifice fly and spark a three-run burst, but that was it for the Giants' offense.

The Senators rallied to win the game 4-3 in 12 innings. Worst of all, their last three runs scored on a couple of bad-hop groun-ders and major gaffes. With the Giants still

leading 3-1 in the eighth, Harris's grounder took a bad hop over Lindstrom's head and two runs scored. In the eleventh right-hander Walter Johnson struck out Frisch and Kelly with a runner in scoring position, as McGraw watched helplessly from the dugout. One can only guess his feelings in the twelfth. Washington's Muddy Ruel started the trouble by popping up behind the plate. Easy out? New York catcher Hank Gowdy snagged his foot in his own discarded mask. Caught like a rabbit in a trap, he shook his leg futilely, then lunged; the ball dropped safely. (Perhaps McGraw was thinking of Fred Merkle.) Ruel then doubled to left. If that wasn't humiliating enough, Johnson batted for himself and reached first when Travis Jackson fumbled a grounder. (Maybe McGraw was remem-bering Fred Snodgrass). The crowning blow came when Earl McNeely grounded to third and, almost unbelievably, the ball took another bad hop over Lindstrom's head to score Ruel with the winning run. (Recalling another debacle involving a blameless third baseman, McGraw might have had visions of poor Heinie Zimmerman.) All in all, it was a finish like the old joke: "Cheer up – things could be worse. So he cheered up and, sure enough, things got worse."

Top: *New York shortstop Travis Jackson, a corker for 15 seasons, steals a base in the 1924 Series.*

Above: *Washington's Goose Goslin is thrown out at first on a great play by Travis Jackson in the 1924 Series opener. The first baseman taking Jackson's throw is Bill Terry.*

Above: *Mel Ott, rightfielder supreme.*

Above far right: *John McGraw (l) and Rogers Hornsby. Their troubled relationship lasted only one year; despite batting .361, Hornsby was traded to the Braves.*

Right: *Frankie Frisch had a career batting average of .316.*

In the following seasons, McGraw's house of cards collapsed around him. Despite seven future Hall of Famers on the roster, the club, increasingly second fiddle to the Yankees both in the standings and in the eyes of the fans, suffered on and off the field. The years passed much too slowly:

1925 – McGraw gets sick and misses two weeks of spring training. The Giants finish second to Pittsburgh. Christy Mathewson dies of tuberculosis during the World Series. McGraw's mind is as sharp as ever, though. He signs a scared 16-year-old catcher named Mel Ott and switches him to rightfield. Twenty-two seasons later Ott retires after mastering the Polo Grounds' tough rightfield wall and homering 511 times. Knuckleballer Freddie Fitzsimmons, known for his "turntable" delivery, signs on and gets the first of 170 wins as a Giant.

1926 – While the Giants finish fifth, Meusel and Groh are released and the sore-armed Nehf is traded to the Reds. When Nehf learns that McGraw didn't inform the Reds of his arm problems, he doesn't speak to McGraw for six years. Even stalwarts like Doyle and Frisch resent McGraw's old-time discipline, and Frisch briefly bolts the team to earn a trade to the Cardinals.

1927 – On the silver anniversary of his first game as Giants manager, McGraw is honored with two silver cups, a silver cane, a silver platter and a silver serving set. The

Giants then lose 8-5 to the Cubs. New York finishes two games behind Pittsburgh in third, while the Yankees win the Series with perhaps the best team ever assembled. New Giant captain Rogers Hornsby, acquired for Frisch in a malcontent-for-malcontent trade, is sued for unpaid gambling debts. Though he bats .361, Hornsby feuds with club president Stoneham and several teammates. Some consolations: Newcomer Burleigh Grimes wins 13 straight and Terry is among the league leaders with 20 homers, 13 triples, and 121 RBIs.

1928 – McGraw trades Hornsby and holdout Grimes, who then have much better seasons than their forgettable replacements. The Giants hang in the race until September 27, when a bad call by Bill Klem cost them a big game. They again finish two games out. After Lindstrom wishes McGraw a broken leg for fining him, McGraw does just that; he is hit by a cab and breaks a leg. One of McGraw's "private eyes," Dick Kinsella, breaks away from the Democratic convention in Houston to sign a young screwball pitcher by the name of Carl Hubbell.

1929 – McGraw encourages Hubbell to throw his unusual pitch, and he hurls an 11-0 no-hitter against the Pirates. Hubbell's buddy Ott, taking the characteristic high-stepping swing that McGraw loves, supports Carl with two homers. On the next to last day of the season Ott and Philadelphia's Chuck Klein enter a doubleheader tied for the league lead with 42 homers. Klein hits one out in his first at bat to break Hornsby's NL season record. Phillie manager Burt Shotton orders Ott walked his last five times up that day – once with the bases loaded. Ott is held to two singles the last day and loses the title 43-42. The Giants finish third, 13½ games out. Rejected club secretary Francis X. McQuade and the club exchange acrimonious legal suits, McQuade eventually losing both his job and back pay.

1930 – The Giants, still in third, get a boost from Lindstrom, Terry, Ott and Hubbell; their teammates don't fare as well. In a particularly sad game – August 24 at Chicago – New York's pennant express is derailed, Lindstrom's 24-game hitting streak is stopped, and the Cubs win 3-2 when Giant reliever Joe Heving takes a full windup while Danny Taylor steals home. For years afterwards, Dan Daniel of the *New York World-Telegram* sighs, "All I can see is Heving holding that damn ball."

1931 – The Giants finish second, 13 games behind St. Louis. Terry loses the batting title by .0003, and his salary is cut 22 percent. After an ejection following a violent

mid-season argument with an umpire, McGraw is fined $150 and suspended – for the first time in 10 years – by NL president John Heydler.

The McGraw era ended in 1932, but not without a sentimental touch. Art Nehf, the sore-armed pitcher McGraw had traded to the Reds six years earlier, showed up at spring training with a husky young outfielder named Hank Leiber in tow. Asked why he was recommending a player to a manager he'd been feuding with, Nehf said, "It's curious, the grip McGraw gets on you. My other managers were fine men who treated me well but when I had a ballplayer I knew could make the big leagues, I had to

Above: *Carl Hubbell's pitches looked even stranger than his windup: The Hall of Fame screwballer struck out five immortals in a row in the 1934 All-Star Game.*

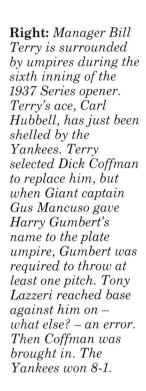

Right: *Manager Bill Terry is surrounded by umpires during the sixth inning of the 1937 Series opener. Terry's ace, Carl Hubbell, has just been shelled by the Yankees. Terry selected Dick Coffman to replace him, but when Giant captain Gus Mancuso gave Harry Gumbert's name to the plate umpire, Gumbert was required to throw at least one pitch. Tony Lazzeri reached base against him on – what else? – an error. Then Coffman was brought in. The Yankees won 8-1.*

give him to McGraw even though I hadn't spoke to Mac for six years." Leiber hit .288 over 10 seasons with the Giants and Cubs.

Nonetheless, the current Giant players, led by Lindstrom, were in full revolt. McGraw was allegedly using a detective on them – "a snitch, a copper, a lousy stool pigeon," they charged. For his part, McGraw was almost powerless to respond. He was now suffering from ptomaine poisoning and constant sinus trouble. "Mrs McGraw, your husband is a very sick man," the family doctor told McGraw's wife Blanche.

McGraw knew it. When a doubleheader was rained out on June 3, he called Terry into his Polo Grounds office. The two hadn't spoken since near-batting champion Terry held out in spring training, finally settling for a $5,000 cut to $18,000. "Sit with your back to the wall," McGraw said. Then: "How would you like to be manager of this ball club?"

Terry was "almost floored," as he later told author Joseph Durso. McGraw went on: "I'm quitting. I want you to think it over for a few days before answering."

"No, no, Mr. McGraw," said Terry, recovering nicely, "I'll take it right now."

So McGraw retired with 10 pennants, 3 world championships and 10 second-place finishes in 29 full seasons with the Giants and a reputation, still intact, as the greatest manager in baseball history.

Was there life after McGraw? Terry's debut was spectacular: a doubleheader sweep of the Phillies that moved the Giants out of last place. Despite some stellar performances, such as Terry, Ott, and Linstrom homering on consecutive pitches August 13, they finished no higher than sixth. Whereupon, Terry started dealing. On October 10 the Giants traded four players for Cardinal catcher Gus Mancuso and right-hander Ray Starr. In a three-club deal with the Phillies and Pirates two months later, New York dispatched Lindstrom (who was unhappy he hadn't been named McGraw's replacement) and outfielder Chick Fullis and landed pitcher Glenn Spencer and outfielder George "Kiddo" Davis.

The underdog Giants went on to play peppery ball and win the 1933 pennant. What personified the season was a July 11 telegram to the team from injured shortstop Blondy Ryan. It read: "They cannot beat us. Am en route." The telegram became the team watchword and Ryan the team spark plug. "Prince Hal" Schumacher went 19-12. But the headliners were Ott, who contributed 23 homers and 103 RBIs, and Hubbell, who led the league in wins (23), shut-outs (10) and earned run average (1.66). After watching Hubbell go ten innings without so much as a 3-2 count, columnist Heywood Broun wrote, "Such control in a left-hander is incredible. There must be a skeleton in Hubbell's closet somewhere, perhaps a *right-handed* maternal grand-mother." In an epic doubleheader sweep on July 2, Hubbell beat the Cardinals 1-0 in eighteen innings, while a wild right-hander named Tarzan Parmelee fanned 13 batters in semidarkness and won a bona fide nightcap 1-0 in only 85 minutes.

The 1933 World Series also resembled a long day's work: The Giants beat the Sena-tors in five games as Hubbell won twice and Ott clinched the finale with a tenth-inning tater. The winning pitcher was Cuban-born Adolfo Luque, the first Hispanic to star in the majors. Afterwards, McGraw threw a party for "his" Giants. He wasn't being en-tirely facetious: McGraw, remember, had ordered Terry to stop pitching, saved Ott's unique batting style from revisionist coach-ing and put him in rightfield, and made a giant as well as a Giant out of Hubbell by encouraging him to throw the scroogie.

The next year McGraw died at age 60. "I owe everything I have to him." said Terry. Others recalled McGraw's unpublicized charity toward needy ex-players and tol-erance of mistakes by young ones. In 1934 something seemed to go out of the team, although it contended as usual. A public-relations blunder didn't help. Questioned about the Dodgers at the winter meetings, Terry joked, "Are they still in the league?" Infuriated, the Dodgers beat the Giants in the last two games of the 1934 season which cost them the pennant. But the season did include another memorable performance by Hubbell. In the All-Star Game he struck out five future Famers in a row: Ruth, Gehrig, Foxx, Simmons, and Cronin.

Despite getting another crack shortstop, Dick "Rowdy Richard" Bartell, the Giants blew another lead to finish third in 1935. In 1936 and 1937, however, they came from behind to take pennants. And what a cast of stars the 1936 team had! Terry singled, doubled and tripled with a bad knee to win a big game, Ott led the league with 33 homers and 135 RBIs, and Hubbell – now called the Meal Ticket – led the Giants from 11 games back by winning his last 16 de-cisions. But what a constellation the Yankees were! After winning a pennant by 19½ games, they beat Hubbell in the pivo-tal fourth game and won the Series in six games.

It was an era of imaginative managing, and few managed with more flourish than Bill Terry. With the Giants trailing the Cubs by seven games in early August of 1937, Terry brought Ott in from rightfield to replace weak-hitting Lou Chiozza at third and inserted Jimmy Ripple in the out-field. Behind the late-season heroics of Ott and Ripple, the Giants took first for good in early September. Unfortunately, the Series was a near-repeat of 1936: the Yankees in five, with Hubbell the only Giant winner.

Hubbell's pitching peaked in 1937, and so did the Giants. Though they led the league for the first half of the 1938 season, they finished five games out in third place – and wouldn't get that close for the next 12 years. By now the Giants were more concerned about the uppity Dodgers in their own

Below left: *Harold Schumacher warms up in preparation for 1933 spring training. "Prince Hal" went on to post a 19-12 record and win a game in the World Series.*

Below right: *Player-manager Bill Terry crosses the plate after homering in the fourth game of the 1933 Series.*

league than the lordly Yankees in the other. So heated was the Giant-Dodger rivalry that words like disgust and fisticuffs were inadequate to describe it: You could add murder. It seems a Dodger partisan named Robert Joyce killed Giant fan Frank Klug when Klug teased him during a Dodger loss.

In 1939 the Giants had epic fights with everyone from Dodgers to umpires. Second baseman Burgess Whitehead was so distressed by a suspension that he asked the *Yankees* for a tryout. The Giants brought up promising pitcher Tom Gorman, who hurt his arm after four no-decisions and went on to a fine career – as an umpire. And, oh yes: Despite a six-player trade, New York slipped to fifth and the third-place Dodgers finished ahead of them for the first time in seven years.

The Giants leveled off at sixth and fifth in 1940 and 1941, bringing the Terry stewardship to a sad close. Ott replaced him as manager in 1942 and got a quick lift when Ott and slugger Johnny Mize, late of the Cardinals, hit homer after homer to propel the pitching-poor Giants to third. But when the Giants lost a disproportionate number of players to World War II, they slipped to dead last in 1943. The lone bright spot was Hubbell's 250th win; after the season he retired and signed a long-term contract to become farm director.

The Giants climbed to fifth in 1944 and 1945 but were last again in 1946, the year several of their players jumped to the "outlaw" Mexican League. And why not leave:

The Giants were quickly becoming the laughingstock of the American baseball fans. Though a record 1,243,773 fans filled the Polo Grounds, they were celebrating peacetime, not Giant baseball. The off-season featured a satirical verse lampooning the club at the annual dinner of the New York baseball writers. Singing to the tune of Bing Crosby's "Swinging on a Star," the writers chanted:

A Giant is a midget, gettin' by on his past,
He can't hit a hook or nuthin' fast,
His club makes money, but it's gone to pot.
The fans go there to dream of Hubbell and Ott.

By most standards the 1947 season could have been viewed as a success. While the Giants climbed to fourth, rookie Larry Jansen went 21-5 and another record gate of 1,599,784 stormed the Polo Grounds to watch the Mize-led "windowbreaking" Giants set a major league season record of 221 homers. Unfortunately, the Dodgers and Yankees overshadowed the Giants by winning pennants of their own. There was more pressure than ever on Ott. Some felt he played for one-run innings by wasting outs with sacrifice bunts; that was fine for teams whose staff could hold leads, but not the weak-armed Giants. Other critics said vaguely that he was "too nice." Midway through the 1948 season the Giants agreed: They replaced Ott with Brooklyn manager Leo Durocher, whose motto was, "Nice guys finish last."

A new era had begun.

Below: *As goes Carl Hubbell, so go the Giants. In his last great season, the "Meal Ticket" won 23 games and led New York to the 1937 pennant. They wouldn't win another for 14 years.*

Below right: *Rightfielder Jimmy Ripple of the Giants scores in game three of the 1937 Series against the Yanks.*

Opposite: *Mel Ott is congratulated by shortstop Dick Bartell after homering to tie game five. Despite Ott's blast, the Yankees won 4-2 to clinch the Series.*

5. The Fight for New York

"Giant fans hated Durocher because he was a Dodger. To drop him suddenly in the Polo Grounds, where the feats of McGraw, Terry, Ott, Matty and the others are a sacred memory, was a shock too abrupt for acceptance."

— Ken Smith in the *New York Mirror*

It was almost unthinkable that a Dodger manager should run the Giants. The teams had been hated foes ever since John McGraw fired Wilbert Robinson back in 1913. By the time Leo "The Lip" Durocher switched teams, the Dodgers were getting the best of the rivalry. Their style, oddly enough, was vintage McGraw: Aggressive baserunning, tight defense, sharp pitching, bench-jockeying – all taught to perfection by the most hated Dodger, Durocher, who had coined "Nice Guys Finish Last" to describe the beloved Ott. By contrast, the Giant style was more casual. The club had been run for years by the distant Stoneham family – the current owner, Horace Stoneham, liked to watch games through binoculars from his centerfield office – and its offense relied almost exclusively on the homer. The Giants' fourth-place finish and the Dodgers' pennant in 1947 testified to a truism: speed, defense, and pitching beat pure power every time.

Right: *Dodger manager Leo Durocher (l) and Giant manager Mel Ott. Why are these men embracing? When Durocher said, "Nice guys finish last," he was referring to Ott. No wonder Giant fans were slow to embrace Leo the Lip when he was chosen to replace Ott in 1948.*

But Giant fans didn't welcome Durocher as their savior; he had rubbed their noses in the dirt too many times. Would Durocher now play Giant ball? Or would the Giants bend to his will?

Durocher had a ready answer. "You, Johnny Mize," he said the day he was hired, "you're no Hal Chase at first, but you're a great hitter and a good ballplayer, and it doesn't look nice for you to lob the ball around the infield. Fire that ball, knock over [Jack] Lohrke or [Bill] Rigney with your throws!"

Durocher knew that the Giants couldn't contend in 1948, and he patiently managed the team to a fifth-place finish. When the Giants could do no better than fifth again in 1949, he became exasperated. It was time to build "my kind of team," he announced. The year featured a flurry of moves. The Giants brought up their first two black players, Hank Thompson and Monte Irvin; sold Mize to the Yankees for $40,000; and traded three players to the Braves for the superb double-play combination of short-stop Alvin Dark and second baseman Eddie Stanky.

By 1950 the Giants were ready to compete with the Dodgers. The rivalry grew fiercer than ever. Forgetting his old loyalty, Durocher would cup his hands around his head to suggest that the Dodgers' Jackie Robinson had a swelled head. "Hey, Leo," Robinson shouted back, "are you still using

Above: *Johnny Mize takes a swing in a spring-training game with the Boston Braves.*

Left: *Intimidating Sal "The Barber" Maglie.*

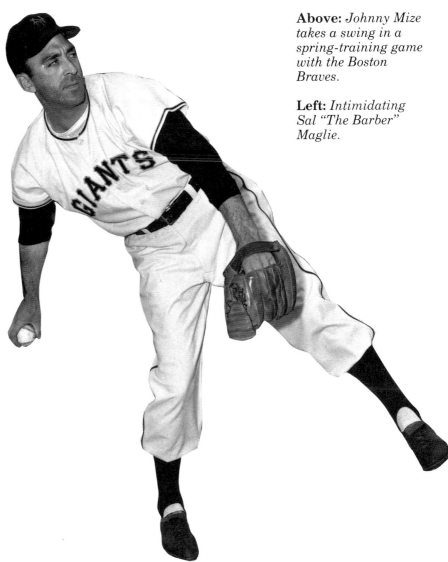

Right: *Willie Mays as a 20-year-old rookie in 1951. After joining the Giants' pennant express, he batted .274, with 20 homers and 68 RBIs in 121 games.*

your wife's perfume?" As Jansen won 19 games, razor-sharp Sal "The Barber" Maglie, reinstated from the Mexican League, went 18-4, and Thomson added 20 homers and 91 RBIs, the Giants finished an impressive third, three games behind the Dodgers and five behind the pennant-winning Phillies. "This proves that I can win anywhere if I have my kind of team," Leo lipped.

Durocher entered the 1951 campaign with a much-feared lineup: first baseman Irvin and third baseman Thompson at the corners; Dark and Stanky in the middle infield; Don Mueller, Whitey Lockman, and Bobby Thomson patrolling the outfield, and a solid-pitching staff superbly handled by catcher Wes Westrum. Hopes were high. So when the Giants lost 11 straight early in the year, Dodger fans were ready to pounce. "Is New York still in the league?" they brayed.

Durocher for one, wasn't panicking. "Let the other clubs talk now, poke fun at us, make wisecracks about us," he said in May. "There is a long way to go before the season is over. We'll show them yet." Just to make sure, Durocher had Lockman and Irvin change positions and replaced Bobby Thomson with a kid hitting .477 at Minnea-polis, Willie Mays by name.

The kid was anything but cocky: Because he had trouble with names, he was forever starting conversations with a tentative "Say, Hey!" At first he had even more trouble with pitching and started out 0-for-12. When Mays begged Durocher to bench him, Leo replied, "You're my center-fielder," whereupon Willie homered off Hall of Famer Warren Spahn. Durocher babied his prodigy, driving him to the park, spending time with him after games. Mays quickly proved he was worth the trouble. In Pittsburgh he made a barehanded catch that Pirate executive Branch Rickey called the best play he'd ever seen – or hoped to see. Mays could do it all: Hit, hit with power, run, field, and throw. Before long he would do it better than anyone.

Mays quickly became a prime ballplayer in the prime of New York City baseball. For the first time in memory, all three New York teams were playing like contenders, and New Yorkers were fervently backing their favorites. The Yankees were so successful they were known as U.S. Steel; those stockbrokers who used to support the Giants were flooding into Yankee Stadium.

Below: In a posed interlude during the Dodger-Giant feud, Brooklyn and Manhattan meet peaceably. From left: Jackie Robinson, Pee Wee Reese, Johnny Mize, Willard Marshall.

Above: *The first all-black outfield in World Series history. From left: Monte Irvin, Willie Mays, Hank Thompson. During the 1951 season the trio had accounted for 52 homers and 222 RBIs.*

The Dodgers were everyman's team – the lovable "Bums" whose radio broadcasts seemed to pour our of every window in Brooklyn. The Giants were cherished by Manhattanites and old New Yorkers pining for the days of Mr. McGraw. And all over the city people were debating the merits of the awesomely talented young centerfielders: the Yankees' Mickey Mantle, the Dodgers' Duke Snider, and the Giants' Willie Mays.

As Giant play picked up in mid-season, Durocher kept tinkering. On July 20 he moved Bobby Thomson to third and Irvin to left. The move, like Bill Terry's mid-season shift of Mel Ott to first in 1937, proved inspirational, but not immediately. By August 11 the Giants were in second, but 13½ games behind the Dodgers with only 44 games remaining. The most famous comeback team, the 1914 Miracle Braves, had been only 3½ out on that date.

But not even the Miracle Braves had a star like Mays. On August 15, with the score 1-1 and the Dodgers' Billy Cox on third, Willie made a wondrous catch, spun around while still running, and fired a 325-foot strike to Westrum to nail Cox at the plate. Then Mays led off with a single and scored when Westrum hit a two-run homer to give the Giants a 3-1 victory. But postgame conversations kept returning to the fielding play. "I was so sure Willie wouldn't bother to make the throw that I didn't even take my mask off," said Westrum. "I won't believe that play can be made until I see it *again*," said Dodger manager Chuck Dressen.

One miracle followed another. The Giants went on to win 16 straight – baseball's longest streak since 1916 – and sliced Brooklyn's lead to five. Don Mueller hit five home runs in two games to set a league record. Suddenly the Dodgers were panicking. As the Giants won an incredible 39 of their last 47 games – staging, by all odds, the greatest comeback in baseball history – the Dodgers were struggling to play .500 ball. Indeed, it took an amazing diving stop and clutch homer by Jackie Robinson on the last day of the season to produce a dead-heat finish between the two teams.

So the pennant had to be decided by a best-of-three playoff – and another incredible Giant comeback. In the opener the Giants' Jim Hearn beat Ralph Branca 3-1. Brooklyn rebounded to win 10-0 behind Clem Labine. Then came perhaps the most celebrated and second-guessed game ever.

The scene: The Polo Grounds, October 3, 1951, Maglie vs. Don Newcombe. As 34,320 fans looked on, the Dodgers took a seemingly insurmountable 4-1 lead into the ninth. Now watch the bouncing ball and listen to the critics. Al Dark led off by singling between first and second. Dodger first baseman Gil Hodges held him close (*Why? Dark was no threat to steal with his team*

three runs down!) and sure enough, Don Mueller singled in the large gap on the right side of the infield, moving Dark to third. Newcombe induced Irvin to pop up, but Lockman doubled to left, Dark scoring and Mueller injuring his ankle as he slid safely into third. Clint Hartung ran for him.

Dressen replaced Newcombe with Branca (*Why not Carl Erskine or Clem Labine?*) and told him to pitch to Bobby Thomson (*Why not walk the noted Branca-basher to set up a force at every base and pitch to the visibly nervous rookie, Mays?*). Branca threw a fastball for a called strike one. Let Giant radio announcer Russ Hodges describe what happened next:

"Branca throws . . . there's a long drive . . . It's gonna be, I believe . . . THE GIANTS WIN THE PENNANT! THE GIANTS WIN THE PENNANT! THE GIANTS WIN THE PENNANT! Bobby Thomson hits into the lower deck of the leftfield stands. THE GIANTS WIN THE PENNANT! THE GIANTS WIN THE PENNANT AND THEY'RE GOING CRAZY! THE GIANTS WIN THE PENNANT! THE GIANTS WIN THE PENNANT!"

Thomson had indeed hit one to the short porch in leftfield produced by the Polo Grounds' oblong dimensions, and the fans were indeed going crazy. As the Dodgers walked trance-like to their clubhouse in distant centerfield, teammates mobbed Thomson at the plate, and Durocher and Stanky rolled in the grass together down the third-base line. The homer, would forever be known as the "Shot Heard 'Round the World" and the season "The

Top left: *Bobby Thomson, the "Staten Island Scot," who was born in Glasgow, batted .293, with 32 homers and 101 RBIs, during the 1951 season. The last homer will live forever.*

Bottom left: *Thomson heads for home after hitting his celebrated "Shot Heard 'Round the World" – the 3-run, ninth-inning, come-from-behind playoff homer that won the 1951 pennant. Many consider it the most dramatic moment in baseball history.*

Miracle at Coogan's Bluff."

Alas, no miracle can be sustained forever. The AL champion Yankees beat the Giants in an anticlimatic World Series, four games to two.

It would be three seasons before the Giants won another pennant. In 1952 they finished second to the Dodgers after Irvin broke an ankle and Mays was called into the service for the Korean War. The Giant-Dodger feud waged interminably, Durocher and Dressen matching wits, the teams averaging 27 minutes longer to play each other than other league games took. Mays was still gone in 1953, and the Giants fell back to fifth; the pitching of rookie Ruben Gomez (13-11) was virtually the season's only good news. Meanwhile, the Giant-Dodger rivalry reached new heights – or depths – when Brooklyn's Carl Furillo reacted to being hit on the wrist by racing into the Giant dugout and trying to start a fight with Durocher. In a season otherwise reminiscent of the early 40s, the Giants were out of contention in August. "The Giants," said Dressen, "is dead."

But in 1954 they were a pretty lively corpse. Mays returned stronger than ever: The league's Most Valuable Player won the batting title with a .345 average while homering 41 times. Johnny Antonelli, acquired from the Braves for Bobby Thomson, won 11 straight and went 21-7, with a league-leading 2.29 earned run average. Gomez (17-9), Maglie (14-6), Marv Grissom (10-7 and 19 saves) and Hoyt Wilhelm (12-4 and 7 saves) gave the team unaccustomed pitching depth. And, yes, the Giants won the pennant!

Even so, they appeared to be no match for the AL champion Cleveland Indians, who had set a league mark by winning 111 games. But this was to be another season of miracles at Coogan's Bluff. In game one of the Series the score was tied at 2-2 in the eighth inning with no out and Indians leading off first and second, when the Tribe's Vic Wertz hit a drive to the deepest park of the Polo Grounds. Giant fans held their breaths. In one of the most replayed scenes in baseball history, Mays turned around and raced back, back, back, lost his cap, caught the ball as it passed over his left shoulder, spun, threw to Davey Williams at second, and fell down. In the top of the tenth Mays made a play he later called even better, when he held Wertz to a double instead of an inside-the-park homer by making a barehanded stop. More drama still? In the bottom of the inning pinch hit-

Below: *The prospective Giant infield, entering the 1952 season. From left: Third baseman Bobby Thomson, shortstop Alvin Dark, second baseman Davey Williams, first baseman Whitey Lockman. They could hit as well as field: The foursome had 60 homers in the pennant-winning 1951 season.*

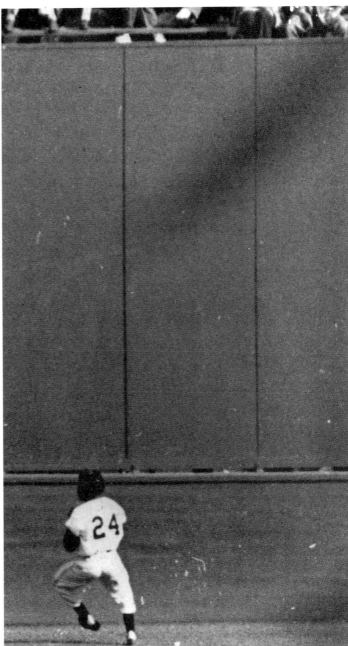

ter Dusty Rhodes won the game 5-2 with a 260-foot homer that barely cleared the rightfield fence.

Both Rhodes and Mays would be heard from again, and soon. Rhodes tied game two by singling Mays home and later homered for an insurance run in a 3-1 win. All Rhodes could produce the following day was a clutch two-run single, while Mays went 3-for-5 in a 6-2 laugher. The Giants took the finale 7-4 to sweep a Series few expected them to even contend in.

It was the last Series played in the Polo Grounds. In 1955 the Giants wasted Mays's 51 homers, finished 18½ games out in third and had to settle for watching the Dodgers beat the Yankees to take their first world title. Durocher grew irascible and ineffective and his contract wasn't renewed; the old Giant Bill Rigney was chosen to replace him. The Giants finished sixth in 1956, while the Yankees beat the Dodgers in a re-match of the previous fall classic. Then the Giants were sixth again and – egad! – a team from Milwaukee beat the Yankees in the 1957 Series.

From 1947 to 1957 a New York team won the pennant 10 out of a possible 11 times. The Yankees won nine pennants and seven Series, the Dodgers six pennants and one Series, and the Giants two pennants and one Series. But after the 1957 season the Dodgers and Giants, having tried in vain to negotiate substantial city financing for new stadiums, left for Los Angeles and San Francisco, respectively. On September 29, 1957, the third-place Giants lost to the Pirates 9-1 before only 11,606 fans to close out their Polo Grounds era. Many old Giants watched the finale with McGraw's widow Blanche. "This would have broken John's heart," she said.

The fight was over; all New York had lost.

Above: *Two views of the most celebrated catch in World Series history. In the eighth inning of the 1954 opener with Cleveland, Giant centerfielder Willie Mays outruns Vic Wertz's long drive, catches the ball (l), and turns to throw quickly to the infield (r), saving 2 runs. The Giants won 5-2 in ten innings and went on to sweep the Series.*

6. Go West, Young Men

The Giants couldn't have asked for better expansion territory than San Francisco. The City by the Bay, internationally known as a bastion of culture, also boasted a sparkling baseball tradition. For 99 years the national pastime had been played off and on in San Francisco. The citizens were hip to every nuance of the game: They had even coined the term "sandlot."

They quickly began explaining the origins of the term to the Giants. In 1850 a triangular lot created by sand had been designated for use as a cemetery. Over the next 20 years the Board of Supervisors got permission to remove the dead in order to level the hill for construction of a park, and subsequently to replace the park with a new city hall. Between park and public building, the "Sand-Lot," as it was known, became a training ground for ballplayers. Local sportswriters called them "sand-lotters," and the terms "sandlot" and "sand-lotters" came to connote amateur and semi-pro play everywhere.

In 1859 some young tradesmen and mer-

chants who had immigrated from the East formed the first Bay Area team, the Eagle Baseball Club. The region's first game was played at Centre's Bridge, on Washington's Birthday 1860, between the Eagles and Red Rovers – and it immediately set a standard for excitement and controversy. With the score tied at 33 after nine innings, the Red Rovers claimed the Eagles pitcher was using an illegal delivery and stalked off the field, forfeiting the game.

By the late 1860s the Eagles were getting stiff competition from almost two dozen local teams. In 1869 the country's first openly professional nine, the Cincinnati Red Stockings, came to the area on their celebrated nationwide tour. The Red Stockings promptly routed the Eagles 35-4 and 58-4 before whipping a couple of other local clubs. Cincinnati left, and so, for the time being, did respectable baseball. For the next decade games were interrupted by everything from fights to gamblers shooting off guns as a means of distracting the participants.

In June of 1879 some 4,000 people

Below: *The Giants played in San Francisco's intimate Seals Stadium while Candlestick Park was under construction in 1958 and 1959. The land Seals Stadium stood on was previously the site of an ore deposit called Home Plate Mine.*

watched a game between the Knickerbockers and Eagles at the San Francisco Rec Grounds. The attraction: Eastern pros Billy Barnie and Edward "The Only" Nolan. The same year former Red Stocking Cal McVey and his Bay City team stunned the Chicago White Stockings by winning four of six games in an exhibition series. In subsequent seasons the California game faced some familiar 19th-century problems – inebriated players, athletes jumping teams, teams jumping leagues. By the 1890s Bay Area teams either played independently or dropped in and out of the loosely run California League and its rival, the California State League. In the middle of the decade both leagues suspended operations. To restore sanity the *San Francisco Examiner* inaugurated a tournament for players 18 and under – a forerunner of American Legion baseball.

The Pacific Coast League formed in 1903 and eventually became the strongest minor league in the country. It not only produced countless major leaguers but an excellent baseball tradition of its own. In 1933 Joe DiMaggio ran off a 61-game hitting streak for the San Francisco Seals; eight years later he would go on to greater things in the majors. What's more, the PCL rivalry between the Seals and Oakland Oaks proved every bit as heated as the Giant-Yankee and Giant-Dodger matchups. On many a Sunday the Oaks and Seals staged morning-afternoon doubleheaders – a 10 A.M. game in Oakland's 12,000-seat Oaks Park, followed by a ferry ride and an afternoon tilt at 23,741-seat Seals Stadium. At the height of the rivalry, in 1946, the PCL-champion Seals drew a league-record 670,563 fans under manager Lefty O'Doul while the Casey Stengel-skippered Oaks drew a healthy 634,311.

The San Francisco Giants played their first two seasons, 1958 and 1959, at Seals Stadium while Candlestick Park was under construction. Many Giants were probably sad to leave Seals Stadium. For one thing, the park was only five minutes from downtown. It had a unique baseball flavor: The land it stood on was previously the site of a mine, and the original deed providentially identified it as "Home Plate Mine." (Baseball country, in-deed.) The ballpark itself was a minor-league classic. Though only 40 percent the capacity of the Polo Grounds, white-concrete Seals Stadium was at once cozy and challenging. The fans were close to the field but the fences were a respectable distance from the plate, with foul lines 365 feet to left and 355 to right and dead-center fully 410 away.

Seals Stadium deserved entertaining games and got them. When the Seals

played the Sacramento Solons in the stadium's minor league finale – a "joyous wake" on September 15, 1957 – people wandered on to the field all afternoon for handshakes and autographs. Non-roster manager Joe Gordon started at second, and outfielder Albie Pearson opened at pitcher and played five different positions. In the second inning Gordon moved to the mound and threw what looked like a strike. "Ball one," said umpire Chris Pelekoudas. Gordon raced to the plate protesting. Pelekoudas responded that Gordon might do better umpiring. Whereupon they switched places! Pelekoudas threw a perfect pitch. "Slow-wow-ball," yelled Gordon.

What a wonderful place: If Seals Stadium could have been expanded to seat 40,000 and had better parking, it would have been an ideal locale for the Giants.

It wasn't exactly a bad interim home. On its major league opening day – April 15, 1958 – Ruben Gomez six-hit the Dodgers

Above: *Seals Stadium boasted a plate-glass backstop made of Tuf-Flex. Supposedly five times stronger than regular plate glass, the backstop endured this pounding by the minor league San Francisco Seals.*

Above: *Giant rookie Orlando Cepeda made a diving tag of a baserunner in 1958. The "Baby Bull" stole the hearts of Bay Area rooters, and it broke their hearts when the Giants traded him to St. Louis in 1966.*

Right: *Willie Mays batting against the Cardinals in his first year on the West Coast. Unlike Cepeda, Mays was not immediately welcomed by Californians, who regarded him as an Eastern interloper.*

8-0, Daryl Spencer hit the stadium's first big-time homer, and rookie Orlando Cepeda added another circuit blast. The excitement didn't slip all season: The Giants went on to average almost five runs a game, and nine players had ten or more homers. To the special delight of locals, no fewer than six rookies contributed to giving the transplanted team a California flavor: Jim Davenport, Bob Schmidt, Willie Kirkland, Felipe Alou, Leon Wagner, and Cepeda. "The Baby Bull," Cepeda, who hit .312 and had 25 homers and 96 runs batted in, was Rookie of the Year and a great fan favorite. And there was more fun still when the Giants took 16 of 22 from the Dodgers and drew a city-record 1,272,625 into their bandbox.

In the midst of such a spirited beginning, it was easy to overlook that the Giants virtually patented the term June Swoon by going 10-16 in the marriage month and dropping from first to third. "If we had any kind of pitching, we would have won the pennant by a dozen games," crowed owner Horace Stoneham. He immediately traded for Jack Sanford and Toothpick Sam Jones – needed additions to a staff that had relied on Johnny Antonelli (16-13) and league ERA champ Stu Miller (2.47). Looking forward to 1959, Stoneham boasted, "I don't even miss Broadway."

Oddly, the Giants' best player probably did. Though he hit for his best average (.347), with 29 homers and 96 RBIs, Willie Mays was not warmly welcomed in San Francisco. As far as Bay Area fans were concerned, the only centerfielder who ever lived was their own Joe DiMaggio. Mays, neither a local product nor a quintessentially-San Francisco man-about-town, was merely the best all-around player in the history of the game.

In 1959 pennant fever waxed early – then waned, this time during a July slump. Needing a lift, the Giants brought up PCL batting leader (.372) Willie McCovey. The 6′ 4″ first baseman, nicknamed "Stretch," debuted July 30 with two singles and two triples off Philadelphia's Hall of Fame pitcher Robin Roberts. With style and flair to accompany his own Hall of Fame talent, Stretch eventually became the most popular player in the history of the franchise.

Boosted by the first of McCovey's 521 homers, the Giants took eight of nine games and held on to a two-game lead with eight dates remaining on the schedule. Alas, the storybook season had a checkbook ending: The Giants couldn't win the money games. They dropped a three-game series to the Dodgers that included the Seals Stadium finale and had to settle for repeating in third. At least they had some pitching for

Above: *Willie McCovey, without a doubt the most popular player in the history of the San Francisco franchise. Fans liked the 6′ 4″ "Stretch" for his mighty homers and sophisticated manner. It was a treat just watching him take his stance, when he dipped his left shoulder, spread his feet wide apart, and waved his bat like a tomahawk.*

Left: *Bill Rigney, who managed the Giants on both coasts.*

Above: *Ed Bressoud tags the Cardinals' Daryl Spencer, who strayed off first in a 1960 game. Bressoud took the throw from pitcher Sad Sam Jones, winner of the Candlestick Park opener and 17 other games that year.*

a change. Jones went 21-15 while leading the league with a 2.83 ERA, Antonelli won 19, and Sanford added 15.

In 1960 the Giants again swooned in June (11-16), dropped to fifth, and sacked manager Bill Rigney for an interim replacement, Tom (Clancy) Sheehan. Fortunately, attention to their play was diverted by the move to Candlestick Park. Sam Jones won the opener by three-hitting the Dodgers 3-1 before a crowd of 42,269. Then Candlestick became a happier park for opponents than tenants. Why? Because the visitors got to leave. When the weather wasn't windy, it was cold. And when the conditions were perfect, there were other problems. The climb from the parking lot to the stadium was known as Cardiac Hill; in the first 13 games of the season there were five heart attacks at Candlestick. "Climbing up from the Candlestick parking lot is a real hazard to persons with heart ailments," pronounced city coroner Henry Turkel.

The park was to become a noose around the Giants' necks – reducing them to league laughingstocks, driving away fans, thwarting their efforts to land promising players. The Giants weren't entirely to blame for this predicament. In 1954 a $5 million bond issue had been passed to finance the building of the stadium. But there was a catch: Within five years there had to be a major league team to fill it. The catch quickly became a Catch-22: build a great stadium, but attract a team first.

From the beginning the project had been rushed. The city desperately cast about for a location. Downtown was out, because local merchants were opposed and too many residents would have had to be replaced by expensive eminent domain. A search committee recommended Candlestick Point, where only 8 of the 75 acres necessary to build a 40,000-seat stadium had to be taken by domain because the owner of the remaining 67 acres, Charles Harney, offered to sell the city his land for only $2.7 million. The future looked too good to be true. It was.

Harney, who supervised construction, assumed the stadium would be named after him. When he learned otherwise he backed out of the project before completion. No wonder the park opened a season late.

In fairness, Candlestick was the first stadium built since the Depression; as a modern style-setter, it had to be constructed without the advantage of precedent. Understandably, it turned out to be an uneven product – nicely equipped for television and lighting, but housing a heating system that didn't function as promised. Furthermore, San Francisco is a windy city in many neighborhoods. In fact, Antonelli's anger over two wind-aided homers in Seals Stadium contributed to his departure in 1961.

To their credit, the Giants contended that year despite the ongoing stadium controversy. Under rookie manager Alvin Dark they finished a respectable third. Mays (.308, 40 homers, 123 RBIs) began getting grudging support from the fans. Unfortunately, the pitching woes returned. The team's biggest winner (14-5) and save leader (17) was Stu Miller. In the All-Star Game, scheduled at Candlestick to showcase the new franchise and stadium, Miller was literally blown off the mound. Clearly the Giants looked forward to better days.

Left: *Alvin Dark (r) at the 1960 press conference announcing his appointment as Giant manager. Two years later the "Swamp Fox" managed the Giants to their first West Coast pennant. Club vice president Chub Feeney is seated next to Dark.*

Below: *Candlestick Park before the Giants opened there. Looks nice, doesn't it? Unfortunately, the Stick doesn't feel quite so hospitable when the wind blows through.*

7. 1951 Again

The Giants and Dodgers moved west, but their rivalry didn't budge an inch. True to their names, the Giants kept swatting for the long ball, while the Dodgers kept playing shiftier, smarter baseball.

In the early West Coast years there was one glorious exception: 1962. Before the season Giant manager Alvin Dark gave up little of merit to acquire pitchers Don Larsen and Billy Pierce. The result was 21 wins and 12 saves. Added to Jack Sanford's 24 wins, Billy O'Dell's 19, and Juan Marichal's 18, the pickups gave the Giants an unusually strong staff.

The hitting was better than ever. Willie Mays won a home run title with 49 while batting .304 and driving in 141 runs; Orlando Cepeda (.306, 35 HRs, 114 RBIs) and Felipe Alou (.316, 25 HRs, 98 RBIs) were right on his heels; Willie McCovey

homered 20 times in only 229 bats; Harvey Kuenn hit .304 with nine game-winning RBIs; Jim Davenport batted a career-high .297, and catchers Tom Haller and Ed Bailey added 35 taters and 100 ribbies. What a staff! What a lineup!

Nonetheless, it took a little luck and a lot of pluck to win the pennant that year. The Dodgers led the Giants by two games in mid-July when LA's 14-game winner Sandy Koufax was lost – apparently for the season – because of circulatory trouble in his fingers. With Koufax, the Dodgers might have been unstoppable; without him, they were vulnerable indeed.

Nonetheless, the Dodgers were actually leading the Giants by 5½ games when they arrived in San Francisco for a three-game series down the stretch. That's when two strong candidates for Giant MVP – ground-

Below left: *Juan Marichal won an unmatched 191 games in the 1960s. The "Dominican Dandy" used a high-kick delivery that disguised the ball until the last instant, then released it overhand, three-quarters, or sidearm.*

Below right: *Billy O'Dell's 19 wins helped the Giants take the 1962 pennant.*

Left: *Giant manager Alvin Dark (l) wonders if rookie pitcher Bob Garibaldi will make the staff. The righthander got a $100,000 bonus but no wins.*

Below left: *Harvey Kuenn's 3-run double won a September 1962 game against the Dodgers that Dark called the most important he ever managed.*

Below right: *Jim Davenport hit a career-high .297 in 1962.*

Above: *Willie Mays had happier days when the Giant faithful began to accept him in the 1960s.*

keepers Matty and Jerry Schwab – went to work. Like all Giants, they were concerned about LA's speedy Maury Wills. In a pre-dawn trip to the Candlestick infield, the Schwabs installed a 5-by-15-foot speed trap of sand, peat moss, and water near first base. There would be no stealing of second that day; slogging there, maybe. "An aircraft carrier wouldn't have run aground," wrote Jim Murray in the *Los Angeles Times.* "They found two abalone under second base."

The umpires caught on before the game and ordered the Schwabs to make repairs. No fools, they brought in more swamp mix and watered down the area. "What could you do," Tommy Davis, the Dodgers' batting champion that year, remembered. "It was their park. They were going to get away with anything." Unnerved, the Dodgers stole no bases and lost 11-2. Though the Schwabs were forced to undo their dirty work, LA went on to lose the next two games as well.

San Francisco subsequently took a three of four in Los Angeles, winning the finale on Kuenn's three-run double in the ninth. But the Giants weren't home free. With seven games remaining they were four out. "We aren't through," said manager Dark, now known as the Swamp Fox. "The race will go down to the last day."

What he didn't know was that it would go further than that. One game out on the last day of the season, the Giants played Houston, the Dodgers played St. Louis, and fans of both teams listened to their transistor radios. All afternoon Giant broadcasters Russ Hodges and Lon Simmons kept relaying Dodger news to their listeners. Meanwhile, the Giants somehow concentrated on their own game and beat the Astros 2-1 thanks to a Mays homer in the eighth. At the time the Dodger-Card game was only five innings old and scoreless. Transistorized, the Candlestick Park fans didn't budge from their seats; they were listening to the Dodgers game.

Indeed, people were disrupting their routines all over the city. At Kezar Stadium, where the football 49ers were playing the Minnesota Vikings in an otherwise forgettable game, Niner quarterback John Brodie was delighted to hear a great roar erupt when he settled behind the center. He waved for silence. None came: The crowd had just heard the news that Gene Oliver had homered in the ninth to give the Cards a 1-0 victory over the Dodgers.

With the Giants and Dodgers tied at season's end, it was 1951 all over again. And their three-game playoff ended amid almost as much excitement as the "Shot Heard 'Round the World."

In the opener the Dodgers gambled by taking Koufax off the injury list, but he didn't last through the second. Mays hit two homers and Pierce won his 13th home game in a row, throttling LA 8-0. Facing a humiliating finish, the Dodgers – scoreless in their last three dates – overcame a 5-0 deficit to win game two 8-7 when Wills crossed the plate ahead of a strong Mays throw. The series was now even, and the Dodgers had the home advantage in the rubber game.

This time there was ample reason to believe the Dodgers would avenge 1951: They entered the ninth leading 4-2, with redoubtable Ed Roebuck in control. Then the Giants unaccustomedly began chipping away like woodchucks. Pinch hitter Matty Alou led off by singling. One-out walks to McCovey and Felipe Alou loaded the bases. A Mays single off Ed Roebuck's glove made it 4-3 and left the bases still loaded. Stan Williams replaced Roebuck, but the torture continued. Cepeda hit a sacrifice fly to right, tying the score. The Dodgers could have been forgiven for preferring Chinese water torture. Poor Williams threw a wild pitch, walked Bailey to set up a force at the plate, then walked Davenport on five pitches to give the Giants the lead. They went on to win 6-4.

The Giants hadn't rallied from as far behind as the 1951 team. They had gone 103-62 for their best record since the 1913

Left: *In one of many critical Giant-Dodger games during the 1962 season, Tommy Davis steals second while José Pagan takes a high throw. However, the Giants beat the Dodgers 5-1 to take the 3-game series and move 2½ games from the lead.*

Below: *Chuck Hiller is mobbed after hitting a grand slam in the fourth game of the 1962 World Series. The Giants won 7-3 to tie the classic at two games each.*

Above: *Brothers Felipe (l) and Matty Alou were Giant fixtures in the early 1960s. In '62 Felipe was a .316-hitting outfielder and Matty was a productive pinch hitter whose clutch single helped the Giants win the pennant.*

team won 101 times in 152 starts. It was cause for a massive celebration, and San Franciscans did it in typical style. The moment Mays caught the final fly ball and fired it joyously into the Dodger Stadium seats, the "cool, gray city" up the coast went wild. Cars weaved downtown, horns blaring. Some 75,000 fans jammed San Francisco International Airport to greet the returning heroes. Charles Agnews of Grace Cathedral played Handel's "Hallelujah" chorus on the carillon. In the most appropriate symbolic celebration of all, a bar owner named Sam Cohen grabbed a bottle of champagne, ran outside, and poured the contents on the sidewalk: Bubbly literally flowed down the streets.

Unlike 1951, the ensuing Giant-Yankee Series would not be anticlimatic. The Bay Area was clamoring for its first pro champion, and the Series went seven games and 13 days, the outcome riding on a single pitch.

Slugging it out like Ali and Frazier in Manila, the Giants and Yankees traded hard-fought victories. Pow: The Yankees beat the Giants 6-2 in the Candlestick opener behind Whitey Ford. Bam: McCovey homered and Sanford fired a three-hitter to beat the Yanks 2-0 in game two. Biff: With the Series shifting to New York, the Yankees struck for three seventh-inning runs, the Giants countered with two in the

ninth, and New York starter Bill Stafford finally retired Jim Davenport to get an anxious 3-2 win (that pattern would repeat itself). Bop: In the only game approaching a blowout, the Giants evened the Series by beating the Yankees 7-3 on usually light-hitting Chuck Hiller's grand slam. (Trivia note: The win went to Don Larsen on the sixth anniversary of the perfect game he'd pitched as a Yankee.) However, the bloodied winners lost Marichal for the Series when he injured his hand batting in the fifth. Wham: After a day's rain delay the Yankees won game five 5-3 when Ralph Terry beat Sanford and Tom Tresh hit a three-run homer.

Trailing three games to two, the Giants could afford no more losses. Adding to their burden, there was a travel day and a three-day rain delay before the Series could resume at Candlestick. Long layoffs often work to the advantage of the hitters. Not this time. Showing no signs of inactivity, Pierce bested Yankee ace Ford 5-2 on a nifty three-hitter.

October 16, 1962 – a day the Giants recall with longing, regret, and some considerable pride. Say this for them: They didn't go down in flames. In the best kind of Series finale, the Yankees and Giants played a tight, tense game, New York's Ralph Terry and San Francisco's Sanford laying zeroes across the scoreboard like eggs in a henhouse. The Yankees managed to break up the scoreless tie when Tony Kubek's double-play grounder produced a run in the fifth. Then the zeroes started mounting again.

The Giants entered the ninth trailing 1-0. In another crack pinch-hit, Matty Alou beat out a bunt single. Felipe Alou and Chuck Hiller went down swinging. With the Giants out of outs, Mays slashed a shot down the rightfield line. Tie game? As Mays sped to second and Alou to third, Yankee rightfielder Roger Maris alertly cut off the ball and fired it to second base-man Bobby Richardson. Giant third base coach Whitey Lockman faced a monumental decision about sending Alou home. Respecting Maris's good work, he decided to hold the runner at third.

At this point the Giants couldn't have asked for a better batter than Willie McCovey. He was always a good clutch hitter, and Yankee starter Terry was plainly tiring. Sure enough, Terry threw, and McCovey hit a hard line drive between first and second. If it dropped safely, the Giants would win the Series. If it was caught, the Yankees would repeat as Series champions. Never before had a Series boasted a moment of such exquisite torture.

There was only one obstacle to the Giants' first world title on the Coast: second baseman Richardson. Before the at bat Richardson had glanced to the dugout for help on positioning. Manager Ralph Houk looked down, in effect telling Richardson, "you decide." He knew that McCovey was a dead pull hitter who socked the ball with tremendous topspin, and that Terry would probably be throwing slow stuff this late in the game. Therefore, Richardson moved a few steps toward first. But he had more than the laser shot to contend with.

Before McCovey's fatal at bat, shortstop Tony Kubek told Richardson, "I sure hope they don't hit the ball to you."

"Why?" said Richardson.

"Well I'd hate to see you blow it at this time," Kubek joked. Richardson's response was to wish more than ever for the ball to be hit his way.

Below: *Yankee second baseman Bobby Richardson forces Orlando Cepeda in the 1962 World Series.*

Left: *Willie McCovey homers in the second game of the 1962 Series. Number 44 had 18 career grand slams in his 22-year career.*

Just before the pitch, the second-base umpire said, "Hey, Rich, I'd like your cap after the game for my little cousin." That too was on Richardson's mind.

Despite these distractions, Richardson was on the balls of his feet ready to make a move when McCovey hit his smoking drive. Moving left a couple of feet, Richardson reached up and snagged the ball, making the catch look easy. It wasn't. "I thought for a second it would be a hit because of its height off the bat" Richardson told author David Falkner, "but I picked up that top-spin right away . . . I was ready. I was on my way off the field."

So, all too soon, was McCovey. A good

man in defeat as well as victory, he headed downtown to hear some jazz. According to Art Rosenbaum and Bob Stevens, the authors of *The Giants of San Francisco*, Duke Ellington's orchestra noticed Stretch in the audience and played a Duke classic. Only they changed the name to "You Hit It Good, And That Ain't Bad."

Other Giant fans took the loss much harder. In fact, for the next 27 years – the time that would pass before the Giants played in another World Series – San Franciscans brooded over one key moment. "What would have happened," they asked, "if Lockman had given Alou the green light and sent him home on Willie's double?"

8. Boos by the Bay

Q: What do Michael Jackson and the Giants have in common?
A: They both wear gloves on one hand, for no apparent reason.

The Giants didn't become a joke overnight. On the contrary, for the rest of the 1960s they unfailingly won at least 88 games a season. But there was always something to take the glow off their record.

Though Willie McCovey (44 homers, 102 runs batted in, and a major league best 24-game hitting streak) and Juan Marichal (25-8, 2.41 earned run average), became full-fledged stars and Willie Mays had a day in his honor the 1963 Giants never contended after June and finished third with an 88-74 record. Billy Pierce (3-11) was especially disappointing. The hard-luck Marichal, who would win more games (191) in the 1960s than anyone, never did receive an annual Cy Young Award for pitching excellence.

This time he was topped by LA's Sandy Koufax, even though Juan threw the team's first no-hitter in 34 years, a 1-0 whitewashing of Houston. Marichal also beat the Mets' Warren Spahn 1-0 over 16 innings in what may have been the best-pitched game in San Francisco history. The season should also be remembered for the September 10 game in which Jesus, Matty, and Felipe Alou played – the first time three brothers appeared in the same team's batting order in big-league history.

There were good reasons to cheer the 1964 season. Behind Marichal's 21 wins, May's 47 homers, rookie Jim Ray Hart's 31 downtowners, and an 8-6, 23-inning win over the Mets in baseball's longest (7 hour, 23 minutes) game, the Giants went a strong 90-72. On August 24 a crowd of 36,034 in Los Angeles gave Mays two standing ovations for catches considered better than his 1954 grab of the Vic Wertz drive. Reliever Masanari Murakami, the first Japanese to play in the big leagues, threw eleven scoreless innings in his first five games.

Below: *San Francisco became the first team to use three brothers in one game when Jesus (l), Matty (c) and Felipe (r) Alou batted in the eighth inning of the Giants–Mets game on September 10, 1963.*

Above left: *A student of Ted Williams's, Willie McCovey adopted an uppercut swing similar to that used by the Splendid Splinter. Wouldn't you know it. They both homered 521 times.*

Above right: *Billy Pierce won 16 games and game six in the 1962 Series.*

Below left: *As a rookie in 1964, Jim Ray Hart homered 31 times.*

Below right: *Traded to the Cardinals in 1966, ex-Giant Orlando Cepeda was the league's Most Valuable Player the very next season.*

Above left: *Ex-Cardinal Ray Sadecki arrived in the 1966 Orlando Cepeda trade and was a much-publicized disappointment (3-7). Hardly anyone noticed when he won 12 games, with ERAs under 3.00, each of the next 2 seasons.*

Above right: *A slugging catcher, Tom Haller was later the Giant general manager.*

But there were equally good reasons to despair. McCovey slumped, and it seemed both he and Orlando Cepeda were best suited for playing first. In an exceptionally close race, the fourth-place Giants were eliminated from contention when the Cubs beat them 10-7 on October 3. What really sullied the season were remarks in a *Newday* story attributed to manager Alvin Dark. Writer Stan Isaacs quoted Dark as questioning the "mental alertness" of his black and Hispanic players. Though Dark denied making the comments, he was replaced after the season by Herman Franks.

From 1965 to 1969 San Francisco finished second every year. In 1965 the Giants got a league-record 17 August homers from MVP Mays (he hit a career-high 52 overall), 39 from McCovey (after he returned from the outfield to first), and a 14-game winning streak, but finished two games behind Los Angeles. The difference may have been Marichal's nine-day suspension for hitting Dodger catcher John Roseboro over the head with a bat.

Wisely, the Giants felt they had to make changes to win a pennant. Unwisely, they made some wrong ones. In December of 1965 they traded Matty Alou to Pittsburgh, and he went on to win a batting title. On May 8, 1966, they traded Cepeda to St. Louis for pitcher Ray Sadecki. This deal – which general manager Chub Feeney

would spend the rest of his career justifying – seemed to make sense at the time. The disgruntled Cepeda still wanted to play first and was unhappy with his low pay, the Giants appeared to have enough power without him, and the team needed pitching strength.

Alas, Sadecki was a bust (3-7, 5.40 ERA), while Cepeda came to life (17 homers, 58 RBIs in 123 games). Only by getting power from Mays (37 homers), McCovey (36), Hart (33), and catcher Tom Haller (27), plus 46 wins from Marichal and Gaylord Perry, did the Giants finish a tantalizing one-and-a-half games behind the Dodgers.

In 1967 Mike McCormick was picked up from the Senators in one of the Giants' best trades. The left-hander responded with a 22-10 record and a 2.85 ERA to win the Cy Young Award. Unfortunately, Perry slipped to 15-17 with nine one-run losses, an ailing Marichal won only 14 times, and an aging Mays (.263, 22 homers) looked downright mortal. A 21-7 record in the stretch gave the Giants a misleading runner-up finish: They were actually 10½ games behind St. Louis. Meanwhile – stick the knife in deeper – Cepeda was the league's Most Valuable Player.

Midway through the 1968 season, Franks announced he would resign if the Giants failed to win a pennant. Whereupon they repeated in second despite the grand slam

start – and not merely because *The Sporting News* named Mays Player of the Decade on January 17. You had to like a club that had signed a player named Alan Mitchell Edward George Patrick Henry Gallagher. Known as "Dirty Al" because he kept diving for balls and getting his uniform soiled, Gallagher was an engaging fixture for the next three seasons.

After replacing King with Charlie Fox early in the 1970 season, the Giants went 67-53 and finished a strong third while McCovey supplied more awesome output (39 homers, 126 RBIs) and Perry won 23 games.

Then came the spectacular, over-achieving 1971 season, one of the most gratifying in club history. For the first time since 1876, the Giants had no .300 hitters, no 20-game winners, and not much of a defense (they led the majors with 179 errors). Yet they won their first NL West title. How? You guessed it: timely execution. On Opening Day Marichal whipped the San Diego Padres 4-0 and Mays homered on the first pitch to him. That was a good omen, and things just got better. The next day short-stop Chris Speier made his major league debut by singling, doubling, and knocking in two runs while Perry won 7-3. After four

Left: *In one of the Giants' better trades, Mike McCormick arrived from Washington in 1967 and led the league with 22 wins.*

Below: *A versatile performer, Bobby Bonds pulled off a rare 30-30 record with 32 homers and 45 stolen bases in 1969.*

rookie Bobby Bonds hit in his debut – a first for this century – Perry's 1-0 no-hitter against the Cardinals, Marichal's 26-9 mark, and a team-record 2.71 ERA.

Why did the Giants do no better than 88-74? For the same reason they couldn't win a title in the 1969 expansion year for yet another frustrated manager, Clyde King; though Willie McCovey had an MVP (.320 and a league-leading 45 homers and 126 RBIs) season, they trailed Atlanta by three games in the new West division with a 90-72 record. And for the same reason they had only one pennant to show for the decade despite averaging 91.4 wins in the last five years. The reason was the team's poor execution.

"Those were good teams, or else we wouldn't have been winning so many games," said Franks, "but the main reason we didn't win a couple of pennants was our double-play combination. I can still remember several games we blew because we couldn't turn the double play."

Said one of the better Giant infielders, Hal Lanier: "We just weren't fundamentally sound. The Giants always waited for the home run. We could hit the long ball with anyone and we had some pretty good pitching, but we never seemed to do the little things we needed to do in the close games."

The 1970s got off to a more promising

Above: *The most celebrated and condemned spitball pitcher of modern times, Gaylord Perry was more skill than saliva. Twice a 20-game winner with the Giants, he won 314 games in his 22-year career.*

games Mays had four homers. After 23 games the Giants were 18-5.

There was much to celebrate – off as well as on the field. On May 6 the Bay Area baseball writers honored Mays's 40th birthday with a big bash, and Irish-tenor manager Fox sang "Willie Boy" to the tune of "Danny Boy." There was so much rollicking fun that the May 29 trade of rookie outfielder George Foster – a move the Giants would later regret – passed little noticed. A five-run eighth inning here, a six-run ninth inning there: the Giants could do no wrong. Behind Bonds's 33 homers and 102 RBIs and Jerry Johnson's 12 wins and 18 saves, they never lost the lead, although Marichal had to beat the Padres 5-1 on the final day to clinch the title.

The party mood continued through the first game of the league playoffs with Pittsburgh. After all, the Giants had beaten the Pirates 9 of 12 times during the season. Make that 10 of 13: McCovey and second baseman Tito Fuentes hit two-run homers and Perry stifled the Bucs 5-4 in the playoff opener. From there, however, it was downhill: The more talented Pirates went on to take three straight, and then won the Series. The Giants went into a 14-year, virtually uninterrupted decline.

Early in 1972 there were signs that things would be different. McCovey suffered a broken arm, Mays was traded to the

Mets, and Perry was swapped to the Indians for another pitcher, Sudden Sam McDowell. An alcoholic, McDowell suddenly became a sad case. The new Giant order was personified by Dave "Kong" Kingman, who would compensate for his tape-measure homers with terrible baserunning, worse fielding, and an unspeakable clubhouse presence. The fifth-place Giants posted a losing (69-86) record for the first time since they moved West.

In 1973 McCovey was back in form (29 homers), Rookie of the Year Gary Matthews hit .300, Ron Bryant went 24-12 and Bobby Bonds (39 homers, 43 stolen bases) established himself as the league's most versatile player. Too much talent, too little team: The Giants (88-74) could do no better than third.

We would do well to rush through the remainder of the 1970s – a luxury the Giants didn't have. They fell to 72-90 and fifth in 1974, when Fox was replaced by Wes Westrum. By now McCovey and Marichal were gone, Foster was about to become a star in Cincinnati, and the Giants had to rebuild with youngsters. Over the next five seasons they won between 71 and 89 games a year, finished third or fourth, and averaged almost a manager a year. Behind the grim team totals were a few moments of mirth, triumph, and virtue:

1975: Ed Halicki threw a no-hitter and another pitcher, John "The Count" Montefusco, was Rookie of the Year.

1976: The Giants remained in San Francisco, but barely. Running out of money, Stoneham sold the club to the Labatt's Brewery of Toronto. San Francisco mayor George Moscone got a restraining order to prevent the transfer. A wealthy financier named Bob Lurie pulled out his checkbook and found he alone could not afford the club. Within minutes of a 5 P.M., March 2, 1976 deadline imposed by the league, Lurie and Arizona cattleman Bud Herseth had pooled their resources to keep the club by the Bay. (Toronto got an expansion franchise.) Crowed Moscone: "Bobby Thomson lives!"

1977: Joe Altobelli was introduced as new Giant manager amid much bewilderment. "They had me confused with Johnny Antonelli and Joey Amalfitano," said Altobelli. "I could have gone to my own press conference with a pad and pencil." McCovey, re-signed after a three-year exile, hit 28 homers and was named Comeback Player of the Year. Gary Lavelle set a club record with 20 saves.

1978: As the third-place Giants drew a respectable 1,740,480 fans for a change, Altobelli was named Manager of the Year and General Manager Spec Richardson, who acquired pitcher Vida Blue (18-10, 2.79 ERA), was selected Executive of the Year. Jack Clark (.306, 25 HRs, 98 RBIs) established club marks with 46 doubles and a 26-game hitting streak.

1979: Bill North stole a team-record 58 bases, and McCovey became the top left-handed slugger in NL history when he hit homer number 512.

Alas, the decade ended in typical Giant form when they made some embarrassing moves. First, they traded third baseman Bill Madlock to the Pirates; he promptly led them to another world title. Altobelli, who was replaced by Dave Bristol, went on to win a world title with Baltimore. And the Giants entered the free-agent sweepstakes by giving Rennie Stennett a ridiculous $1 million signing bonus.

The 1980s began with more of the same when the Giants finished a dismal fifth under their latest skipper, Dave Bristol. At the winter meetings they attracted some attention by sacking Bristol for Frank Robinson, the league's first black manager (he had been the AL's first in 1975). It was felt that Robinson, a hard-nosed Hall of Famer in his playing days, would take the no-nonsense approach the Giants sorely needed. Unfortunately, he and his prime

player, outfielder Jack Clark, feuded endlessly.

The 1981 season was a mixed blessing. It was best known for the mid-season strike, which actually proved to be a boon for the Giants. A struggling 27-32 fifth-place team before the walkout, they went 29-23 after resumption of play. With .300 hitters Jeffrey Leonard and Milt May bolstering sluggers Clark and Darrell Evans, the Giants had the division's fourth best record overall and edged past .500 again.

Racking up the league's strongest second-half record in 1982, the Giants placed third, just two games off the lead, and Robinson was named Manager of the Year. New general manager Tom Haller, who had replaced Richardson during the strike, revamped the rotation by replacing Vida Blue and Doyle Alexander with rookies Atlee Hammaker and Bill Laskey; they combined for 25 wins. In his best season as a Giant Clark had 27 homers and 103 RBIs, while veterans Reggie Smith and Joe Morgan provided punch and leadership, and Greg Minton upped the club save record to 30.

So on to 1983 – and another disappointment. As a number of key players slumped badly, the club dropped to fifth amid fami-

Below left: *Already a Hall of Fame outfielder, Frank Robinson became the first black manager in National League history when he signed with the Giants in 1980. The only Most Valuable Player in both leagues, he was also a two-league Manager of the Year.*

Below right: *Bob Lurie kept the Giants in California.*

liar talk of rebuilding. The next season – well, pre-season – started well when the Giants went 18-9 in spring training. But when the bell rang, the Giants fell into an extended slump and were 16 games out by the All-Star break. Lurie fired Frank Robinson, and interim manager Danny Ozark completed the season while the Giants dropped to last for their first time on the Coast. There was some hope for the future, because Dan Gladden, Chili Davis, and Leonard all hit over .300 to become the league's most promising outfield, and catcher Bob Brenly had 20 homers and 80 RBIs. But 1984 was an old stat story: The Giants were second (.265) in batting and fifth in runs (682) – and last in pitching (4.39 ERA) and defense (173 errors). Not even Lavelle's 77 appearances could bolster the Giant effort.

Could 1985 be any worse? Yes it could. When they traded Jack Clark to St. Louis for pitcher Dave LaPoint, shortstop Jose Uribe, and first baseman David Green, the Giants expected to improve. By batting .080 in his first 21 games, Green quickly became a Sadecki-like scapegoat. In fact, the team had nothing but scapegoats. Not one regular could drive in 63 runs; nary a starter could win nine games. The last non-expansion team to lose in triple figures, the Giants went 62-100 for new manager Jim Davenport and repeated in the cellar. As September finally arrived – and the exiled Clark and his Cardinals were rolling to a pennant – Giant owner Lurie replaced GM Haller with Al Rosen and manager Davenport with Roger Craig.

Though no one sensed it at the time, the Giants were on the road back.

Above: *"Hum, baby":
Roger Craig became
manager in 1985 and
led the Giants back to
greatness.*

Right: *Jack Clark
had 103 RBIs in 1982.*

Opposite: *Shortstop
Jose Uribe's adept
fielding helped
transform the Giants
from a pitching-and-
homer machine to an
all-around team.*

9. Giants Revived

*"Before Roger Craig and Al Rosen took over,
there wasn't much pride in being a Giant.
The players were constantly complaining
about Candlestick Park. Even the uniforms
were ugly, with those orange shirts.*

*"Al and Roger came in and restored Giant
pride. They took the position that we should
consider Candlestick an advantage and that
our opponents were the ones who had to
come in and learn to play there. They got
better uniforms and instituted a dress code.
They also brought in Willie Mays and Willie
McCovey for spring training, and some good
veterans to mix in with the young players."*

– Ex Giant pitcher Terry Mulholland

What a difference new management
can make. When Craig started two
rookies, first baseman Will "The Thrill"
Clark and second baseman Robby Thompson, the 1986 Giants had their first winning
April (13-8) since 1973. Veteran Mike
LaCoss went 9-3 in the first half-season,
and Mike Krukow was strong all season
(20-9). Executing as they rarely had before,
the Giants made 18 successful squeeze
bunts among 101 sacrifices, set a San Francisco record with 143 stolen bases, and won
26 games in their final at bat. The pinch hitters, led by Candy Maldonado's 4 homers
and 20 runs batted in, were the best in the
league.

But what really contributed to the greatest turnabout in club history – they went
from 62-100 and last place to 83-79 and
third – was the change of attitude. Craig, a
former pitcher, coach, and manager best

Left: *Pitcher Mike Krukow went 20-9 in 1986.*

Above: *Kevin Mitchell reached for greatness in 1989 and grabbed himself the Most Valuable Player trophy.*

Right: *In 1989 Rick Reuschel passed the 200-victory plateau and kept going.*

known for teaching the split-fingered fast-ball, was the man responsible.

He had learned from a master. Back when Craig was a struggling 10-24 pitcher for the 1962 New York Mets, the Giants' McCovey had come to bat against him. "Mr. Craig, where would you like me to position the right-fielder?" Mets manager Casey Stengel called from the dugout. "In the upper deck or the lower deck?"

"As a manager Casey had a marvelous way of keeping a club loose," Craig told *The Show*. "His wit, the way he handled the players, really influenced the way I manage my own team." As new Giant manager, Craig immediately created a can-do atti-tude with a catchy rallying cry, "Hum, baby."

Craig's players not only rewarded him with a good season, but a frequently hila-rious one. On September 3, pitcher Terry Mulholland fielded a comeback by Keith Hernandez of the Mets. Mulholland ran toward first to shorten his throw. Unfortu-nately, he couldn't get the ball out of his Wilson A2000 glove: It was lodged between the middle and index fingers. Mulholland thought fast. He thought well. Then he tossed his glove to first baseman Bob

Brenly. After checking to see that the ball was in it, umpire Ed Montague called "out." Everyone at Shea Stadium cracked up, even batter Hernandez. Brenly, though, had one regret: "I should have flipped the glove around the infield."

In 1987 the Giants were the talk of the league. Led by the all-around hitting (.308, 35 HRs, 91 RBIs) of Will Clark and some shrewd acquisitions like pitcher Rick Reuschel, they drew a club-record 1.9 million fans and won their first NL West title in 16 years.

This was one 200-homer team (they hit 205) that *did* win a title. It was not a one-dimensional club, though. With no pitcher winning more than 13 or saving more than 12 games and Clark and outfielder Kevin Mitchell the only regulars hitting .300, there had to be another total team effort. There was: The Giants led the league with a 3.68 ERA, held opponents to a league-low 669 runs, and completed an unmatched 183 double plays. The poor executors of the 1960s and 1970s would have been especially awed by the double-play combination of shortstop José Uribe, Thompson, and ball-hawk Clark.

In the National League Championship Series against St. Louis, the Giants took a three-games-to-two lead when Dave Dravecky and Krukow threw complete-game victories and Jeffrey Leonard drove

the Cardinals crazy with his "flap-down" trot around the bases after homers in the first four games. Then the magic wore out – and so did the season. The Giants were held scoreless the last two games and had to watch the Cardinal-Minnesota World Series on television.

In this levelling era of the common draft, arbitration, and free agency, it's tough for teams to repeat as champions. They need plenty of good performances and good luck. In 1988 the Giants had neither. Though Clark – whose beautiful swing earned him a second nickname, "The Natural" – batted

Above left: *Pitcher Dave Dravecky courageously attempted to return to the Giants after a bout with cancer.*

Below left: *As good a fielder as a hitter, first baseman Will Clark clenches his fist after doubling up the Cardinals' Ozzie Smith.*

Above right: *Righty Scott Garrelts led the league with a 2.28 ERA in 1989.*

Below right: *Lefty Craig Lefferts contributed to the 1989 pennant with 20 saves.*

.282, with 29 homers, 109 RBIs and 100 walks, many teammates were limping or slumping. Clark had too little help at the plate and Reuschel (19-11) too little on the mound; the Giants (83-79) finished fourth. There were few happy memories and even less levity. Hardest hit was pitcher Dravecky, who was lost for the season with surgery to remove a cancerous growth from his pitching arm. (He tried to return a year later, but suffered a career ending broken arm.)

But it's equally difficult to keep a good team down. In 1989 the Giants were a great team. Their stalwarts, Clark and Mitchell, were known as the Pacific Sock Exchange. Clark (.333, 23 HRs, 111 RBIs) was many a thrill, and MVP Mitchell (.291, 47 HRs, 125 RBIs) was Babe Ruth. Or was it Superman: Mitchell even caught a fly ball barehanded.

The Giants, however, were no two-man team. Reuschel (17-8) passed the 200-win plateau, Scott Garrelts was the league ERA leader (2.28), and in-season pickup Steve Bedrosian (17 saves) and Craig Lefferts (20) anchored a superb bullpen. Third baseman Matt Williams reported at mid-season and clubbed 18 home runs.

You couldn't overlook the table-setters, either. The Giants won 61 of the first 83 games in which Robby Thompson and centerfielder Brett Butler scored. Indeed, when they took the division lead on June 17 and headed down the stretch in first place, the entire organization was in for accolades. "No club works harder than the Giants, from the front office down to the batboys," a scout told *Sports Illustrated.* "They're the only team ever to have four guys working each game with headsets. They position the defense on every pitch, and they steal signs. And their pitchers execute scouting reports to perfection. It all stems from the top. Rosen is the only general manager who sits in back of the screen or in his skybox and tells his assistant [Ralph Nelson, who wears a headset] how to position the players."

Even Candlestick was getting praise. "That park is the biggest home-field advantage in the majors," another scout told *SI,* "because no one wants to play there. Don't even look at the flags. The wind swirls in several different directions at once, and balls blow in from the corners."

In all, the Giant package was too much for the NL West: Cracking the two-million mark in home attendance, San Francisco (92-70) won the division by three games over San Diego. And then the Giants were too much for the NL East champion Cubs. As the Giants won the playoff four games to one, Clark batted .650 while staging a historic one-man show.

"Will Clark thrives on pressure," said Brenly. "He likes to be out there when everyone is looking at him, counting on him." In the eighth inning of game five Clark got his wish. The score was tied 1-1, the bases were loaded, and Clark was facing Mitch "Wild Thing" Williams. "I couldn't afford to walk him," said Williams. "I couldn't afford to nibble." With a 1-2 count he threw a high fastball down the middle, and the playoffs were as good as over. Given a meatball, Clark served it into center for a two-run single, and the Giants went on to win 3-2. Somewhere the late Russ Hodges was shouting, "The Giants win the pennant!" Their first since 1962.

Ah, but was there ever a more anticlimatic World Series than the 1989 one against Oakland? It started amid great expectations: the first Bay Area Series, featuring the spiritual heirs of Connie Mack's Athletics and John McGraw's Giants facing each other for the first time since 1913. There were bragging rights to the neighborhood and an ancient grudge to settle: When McGraw knocked the A's as "white elephants," Mack taunted back by adopting the white elephant as his team logo. Oh, ancient rivalry!

It was even possible to hype the Series title. It was officially called the Battle of the Bay, but ingenious citizens were soon suggesting Bay's Ball, the Bart Series (after recently deceased Commissioner A. Bartlett Giamatti), the BART Series (after Bay Area Rapid Transit, though it doesn't quite reach Candlestick Park) – even the Otis Redding Series (for the pop tune *Sittin' on the Dock of the Bay*). The most clever tag of all may have been the Synagogue Series, because Oakland owner Walter A. Haas, Jr. and Giant owner Bob Lurie were both members of Temple Emanu-El in San Francisco.

The A's and the elements put a damper on all this good fun. In game one, the Giants didn't get a runner to third off A's starter Dave Stewart until the ninth and meekly succumbed 5-0. Mike Moore shackled them the next night 5-1. Both Giant starters, Garrelts and Reuschel, recorded just 12 outs before departing.

The Giants needed a break. They had no idea they'd get one that would last 12 days. At 5:04 P.M. on October 17, just as the A's and Giants were preparing to play game three, an earthquake measuring 7.1 on the Richter scale shook Candlestick Park and much of northern California. At first it seemed like great theater, and fans at the

Left: *In the 1989 National League Championship Series Matt Williams batted in a record 9 runs.*

Below: *Tough to keep off base, tougher to keep from advancing, Brett Butler had 23 bunt hits and 31 steals in 1989.*

Above: *A Giant fan reacts to news about the earthquake that rocked San Francisco and cancelled game three of the 1989 Series.*

Right: *Players look for their family and friends after the cancellation is announced.*

Stick let out a great cheer. Then the lights stayed out and news began filtering in from elsewhere. Part of the Bay Bridge, a large section of Oakland's Nimitz Freeway, and 60 buildings in San Francisco's Marina District were destroyed. That was just the local damage. Game three was quickly postponed.

When would it be resumed? When the time was "appropriate," said commissioner Fay Vincent.

There was no appropriate time to face the powerful 1989 A's. When game three was finally played on October 27, Series MVP Stewart was back and so were the A's bats. Game three to Oakland 13-7. And the next night Moore was back. The A's roared off to an 8-0 lead. The Giants cut it to 8-6. With a teammate on base in the eighth, Mitchell launched one of his patented moon shots. Would there be a tie game and something resembling a Series? Rickey Henderson caught the ball at the fence, and the A's went on to win 9-6. End of Series. End of season.

The real baseball casualty of the earthquake may have been a San Francisco franchise. Lurie had announced he would not renew the lease on Candlestick Park when it expired in 1994. On November 7, 1989, the city's voters were asked to decide Proposition P, a ballot measure authorizing construction of a $115 million downtown stadium. Before the earthquake, it had a decent chance of passing. After damage was reported in the billions, a pleasure palace seemed trivial to many: Prop P failed; baseball seemed dead in San Francisco.

The 1990 season began amid speculation about where the Giants would be headed. The mayor and Board of Supervisors had released them from the lease requirement, and they could leave anytime. The leading candidate seemed to be Santa Clara, some 40 miles south, which had a stadium proposal of its own.

Meanwhile, the 1990 season encompassed almost every facet of Giant history: hope, despair, comeback, color, individual excellence. On May 30, they were in last place, 14½ games out and hurting. Will Clark had a bad foot. Outfielder Kevin Bass, a free agent signed out of Houston, would miss 90 games. Already lacking free-agent emigré Craig Lefferts, the pitching staff was so crippled by injuries that Venus de Milo could have tried out.

But a funny thing happened on the way to the cellar: The Giants didn't swoon in June. To the contrary, they won 16 of 17 to start the month, took 4 straight from the first-place Cincinnati Reds in July, and climbed into contention. Suddenly nearly everyone was a hero, including Craig, who expertly juggled the rotation and pulled off surprise strategems like squeeze bunts with two strikes.

The Giants lapsed in late summer and seemed to drop out of contention for good on September 2, when they clubbed 17 hits yet lost to the Mets and fell 10½ behind the Reds. Craig was asked if he had trouble sleeping after losses like these. "Not really," he said. "My wife isn't much of a baseball fan. We have a drink, talk about other subjects, and go to bed." As relaxed as their skipper, the Giants rebounded again; a week and a half later they were only 6 games out of first.

In the end, the Giants finished in third, but it was a memorable third. Jeff Brantley stepped into the closer void and saved 19 games. Rookie John Burkett, a part-time pro-bowler, rolled to a team-leading 14 wins. Mitchell had another banner year (35 homers, 93 RBIs) and was rewarded with a four-year $15 million contract. When Matt Williams recorded a league-leading 122 RBIs, the Giants became the first club since the 1927 Yankees to boast three different league RBI leaders in three straight seasons. The Yankees were named Meusel, Ruth, and Gehrig. The record-matching Giants were Clark, Mitchell, and Williams.

So the Giants retained their image as "all-timers," and whatever ballpark they play in, they maintain their reputation as one of the great dynasties of baseball.

Left below: *In happier, pre-earthquake days, the Giants celebrate winning the National League Championship.*

Right below: *Matt Williams drove in a league-leading 122 runs in 1990.*

Giant TEAM RECORDS

YEAR-BY-YEAR GIANT STANDINGS

Year	Pos.	Record	Games Behind	Manager
1876	6	21-35	26	Cammeyer
1883	6	46-50	16	Clapp
1884	5	62-50	22	Price/Ward
1885	2	85-27	2	Mutrie
1886	3	75-44	12½	Mutrie
1887	4	68-55	10½	Mutrie
1888	1	84-47	0	Mutrie
1889	1	83-43	0	Mutrie
1890	6	63-68	24	Mutrie
1891	3	71-61	13	Mutrie
1892	8	71-80	31½	Powers
1893	5	68-64	19½	Ward
1894	2	88-44	3	Ward
1895	9	66-65	21½	Davis/Doyle/ Watkins
1896	7	64-67	27	Joyce
1897	3	83-48	9½	Joyce
1898	7	77-73	25½	Joyce/Anson/Joyce
1899	10	60-90	42	Day/Hoey
1900	8	60-78	23	Ewing/Davis
1901	7	52-85	37	Davis
1902	8	48-88	53½	Fogel/Smith/ McGraw
1903	2	84-55	6½	McGraw
1904	1	106-47	+13	McGraw
1905*	1	105-48	+ 9	McGraw
1906	2	96-56	20	McGraw
1907	4	82-71	25½	McGraw
1908	2†	98-56	1	McGraw
1909	3	92-61	18½	McGraw
1910	2	91-63	13	McGraw
1911	1	99-54	7½	McGraw
1912	1	103-48	+10	McGraw
1913	1	101-51	+12½	McGraw
1914	2	84-70	10½	McGraw
1915	8	69-83	21	McGraw
1916	4	86-66	7	McGraw
1917	1	98-56	+10	McGraw
1918	2	71-53	10½	McGraw
1919	2	87-53	9	McGraw
1920	2	86-68	7	McGraw
1921*	1	94-59	+ 4	McGraw
1922*	1	93-61	+ 7	McGraw
1923	1	95-58	+ 4½	McGraw
1924	1	93-60	+ 1½	McGraw
1925	2	86-66	8½	McGraw
1926	5	74-77	13½	McGraw
1927	3	92-62	2	McGraw
1928	2	93-61	2	McGraw
1929	3	84-67	13½	McGraw
1930	3	87-67	5	McGraw
1931	2	87-65	13	McGraw
1932	6†	72-82	18	McGraw/Terry
1933*	1	91-61	+ 5	Terry
1934	2	93-60	2	Terry
1934	3	91-62	8½	Terry
1936	1	92-62	+ 5	Terry
1937	1	95-57	+ 3	Terry
1938	3	83-67	5	Terry
1939	5	77-74	18½	Terry
1940	6	72-80	27½	Terry
1941	5	74-79	25½	Terry
1942	3	85-67	20	Ott
1943	8	55-98	49½	Ott
1944	5	67-87	38	Ott
1945	5	78-74	19	Ott
1946	8	61-93	36	Ott
1947	4	81-73	13	Ott
1948	5	78-76	13½	Ott/Durocher
1949	5	73-81	24	Durocher
1950	3	86-68	5	Durocher
1951	1††	98-59	+ 1	Durocher
1952	2	92-62	4½	Durocher
1953	5	70-84	35	Durocher
1954*	1	97-57	+5	Durocher
1955	3	80-74	18½	Durocher
1956	6	67-87	26	Rigney
1957	6	69-85	26	Rigney
1958	3	80-74	12	Rigney
1959	3	83-71	4	Rigney
1960	5	79-75	16	Rigney/Sheehan
1961	3	85-69	8	Dark
1962	1†††	103-62	+ 1	Dark
1963	3	88-74	11	Dark
1964	4	90-72	3	Dark
1965	2	95-67	2	Franks
1966	2	93-68	1½	Franks
1967	2	91-71	10½	Franks
1968	2	88-74	9	Franks
1969	2	90-72	3	King
1970	3	86-76	16	King/Fox
1971	1†††	90-72	+ 1	Fox
1972	5	69-86	26½	Fox
1973	3	88-74	11	Fox
1974	5	72-90	30	Fox/Westrum
1975	3	80-81	27½	Westrum
1976	4	74-88	28	Rigney
1977	4	75-87	23	Altobelli
1978	3	89-73	6	Altobelli
1979	4	71-91	19½	Altobelli/Bristol
1980	5	75-86	17	Bristol
1981	5/3	56-55	§	Robinson
1982	3	87-75	2	Robinson
1983	5	79-83	12	Robinson
1984	6	66-96	26	Robinson/Ozark
1985	6	62-100	33	Davenport/Craig
1986	3	83-79	13	Craig
1987	1	90-72	+ 6	Craig
1988	4	83-79	11½	Craig
1989	1	92-70	+ 3	Craig
1990	3	85-77	6	Craig

*World Champions.
†Tied for position.
††Defeated Brooklyn in pennant playoff.
†††Defeated Los Angeles in pennant playoff.
§First half 27-32; second, 29-23.

SINGLE-SEASON GIANT BATTING RECORDS

Batting Average	Bill Terry	.401	1930
Hits	Bill Terry	254	1930
Home Runs	Willie Mays	52	1965
Runs Batted In	Mel Ott	151	1929
Runs Scored	Bill Terry	139	1930
Singles	Bill Terry	177	1930
Doubles	Jack Clark	46	1978
Triples	Larry Doyle	25	1911
Slugging Percentage	Willie Mays	.677	1954
Bases on Balls	Eddie Stanky	144	1950
Most Strikeouts	Bobby Bonds	189	1970
Fewest Strikeouts*	Don Mueller	7	1956
Extra Base Hits	Willie Mays	90	1962
Grand Slam Homers	Willie McCovey	3**	1967
Total Bases	Bill Terry	392	1930

*400 at bats minimum.
**Performed feat four times (most recent year listed).

SINGLE-SEASON GIANT PITCHING RECORDS

Wins	Mickey Welch	44	1885
Losses	Luther Taylor	27	1901
ERA (162 innings)	Carl Hubbell	1.61	1933
Winning Percentage	Sal Maglie	.818	1950
Strikeouts	Christy Mathewson	267	1903
Saves	Greg Minton	30	1982
Innings Pitched	Joe McGinnity	434	1903
Game Appearances	Greg Minton	78	1982
Games Started	Mickey Welch	65	1884
Shutouts	Christy Mathewson	12	1908

HALL OF FAMERS

Name	Position	Year Inducted
Christy Mathewson	P	1936
John McGraw	Manager	1937
Willie Keeler	OF	1939
Rogers Hornsby	2B	1942
King Kelly	OF	1945
Roger Bresnahan	C	1945
Dan Brouthers	1B	1945
James O'Roarke	OF	1945
Buck Ewing	C	1946
Joe McGinnity	P	1946
Jesse Burkett	OF	1946
Frankie Frisch	2B	1947
Carl Hubbell	P	1947
Mel Ott	OF	1951
Bill Terry	1B	1954
Gabby Hartnett	C	1955
Ray Schalk	C	1955
Bill McKechnie	Manager	1962
Edd Rousch	OF	1962
Monte Ward	SS	1964
Tim Keefe	P	1964
Burleigh Grimes	P	1964
Casey Stengel	Manager	1966
Ducky Medwick	OF	1968
Waite Hoyt	P	1969
Dave Bancroft	SS	1971
Jake Beckley	1B	1971
Rube Marquard	P	1971
Ross Youngs	OF	1972
Mickey Welch	P	1973
Warren Spahn	P	1973
Monte Irvin	OF	1973
George Kelly	1B	1973
Roger Connor	1B	1976
Fred Lindstrom	3b	1976
Amos Rusie	P	1977
Willie Mays	OF	1979
Hack Wilson	OF	1979
Duke Snider	OF	1980
Johnny Mize	1B	1981
Travis Jackson	SS	1982
Juan Marichal	P	1983
Hoyt Wilhelm	P	1985
Ernie Lombardi	C	1986
Willie McCovey	1B	1986
Red Schoendienst	2B	1989
Joe Morgan	2B	1990

GIANT POST-SEASON RECORD

Playoffs

Year	Opponent	Win-Loss
1951*	Brooklyn Dodgers	2-1
1962*	Los Angeles Dodgers	2-1
1971#	Pittsburgh Pirates	1-3
1985#	St. Louis Cardinals	3-4
1989#	Chicago Cubs	4-1

*Tied for First, Playoff for National League Championship.
#National League Championship Series.

World Series

1905	Philadelphia Athletics	4-1
1911	Philadelphia Athletics	2-4
1912	Boston Red Sox	3-4-1
1913	Philadelphia Athletics	1-4
1917	Chicago White Sox	2-4
1921	New York Yankees	5-3
1922	New York Yankees	4-0-1
1923	New York Yankees	2-4
1924	Washington Senators	3-4
1933	Washington Senators	4-1
1936	New York Yankees	2-4
1937	New York Yankees	1-4
1951	New York Yankees	2-4
1954	Cleveland Indians	4-0
1962	New York Yankees	3-4
1989	Oakland Athletics	0-4

ALL-TIME GIANT CAREER BATTING LEADERS

Games Played	Willie Mays	2857
At Bats	Willie Mays	10477
Hits	Willie Mays	3187
Batting Average	Bill Terry	.341
Home Runs	Willie Mays	646
Runs Scored	Willie Mays	2011
Runs Batted in	Mel Ott	1860
Extra Base Hits	Willie Mays	1289
Stolen Bases	George Burns	334
Total Bases	Willie Mays	5907

ALL-TIME GIANT CAREER PITCHING LEADERS

Innings Pitched	Christy Mathewson	4772
Wins	Christy Mathewson	372
Losses	Christy Mathewson	187
ERA (1100+ Inns)	Christy Mathewson	2.13
Strikeouts	Christy Mathewson	2502
Game Appearances	Gary Lavelle	647
Shutouts	Christy Mathewson	83
Saves	Gary Lavelle	127
No-Hitters	Christy Mathewson	2
	Leon Ames*	2

*Won 5-0 in five innings on 9/14/03. Record also includes 4/15/09 game in which he threw 9⅓ hitless innings, lost on seven hits in 13 innings 3-0.

Index

Numbers in *italics* indicate illustrations